THE WAY
PEOPLE
LIVE

Life
During the
Dust Bowl

THE WAY PEOPLE LIVE

Life During the Dust Bowl

Titles in The Way People Live series include:

Cowboys in the Old West
Games of Ancient Rome
Life Aboard the Space Shuttle
Life Among the Aztec
Life Among the Great Plains Indians
Life Among the Ibo Women of Nigeria
Life Among the Indian Fighters
Life Among the Pirates
Life Among the Puritans
Life Among the Samurai
Life Among the Vikings
Life During the American Revolution
Life During the Black Death
Life During the Crusades
Life During the French Revolution
Life During the Gold Rush
Life During the Great Depression
Life During the Middle Ages
Life During the Renaissance
Life During the Roaring Twenties
Life During the Russian Revolution
Life During the Spanish Inquisition
Life in a California Mission
Life in a Japanese American
    Internment Camp
Life in a Medieval Castle
Life in a Medieval Monastery
Life in a Medieval Village
Life in America During the 1960s
Life in an Amish Community
Life in a Nazi Concentration Camp
Life in Ancient Athens
Life in Ancient China
Life in Ancient Egypt
Life in Ancient Greece

Life in Ancient Rome
Life in a Wild West Show
Life in Berlin
Life in Charles Dickens's England
Life in Communist Russia
Life in Genghis Khan's Mongolia
Life in Hong Kong
Life in Moscow
Life in the Amazon Rain Forest
Life in the American Colonies
Life in the Australian Outback
Life in the Elizabethan Theater
Life in the Hitler Youth
Life in the North During the Civil War
Life in the South During the Civil War
Life in the Warsaw Ghetto
Life in Tokyo
Life in War-Torn Bosnia
Life of a Medieval Knight
Life of a Nazi Soldier
Life of a Roman Gladiator
Life of a Roman Slave
Life of a Roman Soldier
Life of a Slave on a Southern Plantation
Life on Alcatraz
Life on a Medieval Pilgrimage
Life on an African Slave Ship
Life on an Everest Expedition
Life on Ellis Island
Life on the American Frontier
Life on the Oregon Trail
Life on the Pony Express
Life on the Underground Railroad
Life Under the Jim Crow Laws

Life During the Dust Bowl

by Diane Yancey

LUCENT BOOKS®

THOMSON

GALE

San Diego • Detroit • New York • San Francisco • Cleveland • New Haven, Conn. • Waterville, Maine • London • Munich

© 2004 by Lucent Books. Lucent Books is an imprint of The Gale Group, Inc.,
a division of Thomson Learning, Inc.

Lucent Books® and Thomson Learning™ are trademarks used herein under license.

For more information, contact
Lucent Books
27500 Drake Rd.
Farmington Hills, MI 48331-3535
Or you can visit our Internet site at http://www.gale.com

LIBRARY OF CONGRESS CATALOGING-IN-PUBLICATION DATA

Yancey, Diane.
   Life during the Dust Bowl / by Diane Yancey.
     p. cm. — (The way people live)
Summary: Discusses the causes and effects of the disastrous dust storms that hit the
Great Plains in the 1930s.
Includes bibliographical references and index.
   ISBN 1-59018-265-0 (alk. paper)
   1. Great Plains—History—20th century—Juvenile literature. 2. Great Plains—Social
conditions—20th century—Juvenile literature. 3. Agriculture—Great Plains—History—
20th century—Juvenile literature. 4. Dust storms—Great Plains—Social conditions—20th
century—Juvenile literature. 5. Droughts—Great Plains—Social conditions—20th
century—Juvenile literature. 6. Farmers—Great Plains—Social conditions—20th century—
Juvenile literature. 7. New Deal, 1933–1939—Juvenile literature. [1. Great Plains—
History. 2. Dust storms—Great Plains. 3. Droughts—Great Plains. 4. Depressions—1929. 5.
New Deal, 1933–1939.] I. Title. II. Series.
   F595.Y36 2004
   978'.033—dc22
                                             2003019407

Printed in the United States of America

Contents

Discovering the Humanity in Us All

Books in The Way People Live series focus on groups of people in a wide variety of circumstances, settings, and time periods. Some books focus on different cultural groups, others, on people in a particular historical time period, while others cover people involved in a specific event. Each book emphasizes the daily routines, personal and historical struggles, and achievements of people from all walks of life.

To really understand any culture, it is necessary to strip the mind of the common notions we hold about groups of people. These stereotypes are the archenemies of learning. It does not even matter whether the stereotypes are positive or negative; they are confining and tight. Removing them is a challenge that is not easily met, as anyone who has ever tried it will admit. Ideas that do not fit into the templates we create are unwelcome visitors—ones we would prefer remain quietly in a corner or forgotten room.

The cowboy of the Old West is a good example of such confining roles. The cowboy was courageous, yet soft-spoken. His time (it is always a he, in our template) was spent alternatively saving a rancher's daughter from certain death on a runaway stagecoach, or shooting it out with rustlers. At times, of course, he was likely to get a little crazy in town after a trail drive, but for the most part, he was the epitome of inner strength. It is disconcerting to find out that the cowboy is human, even a bit childish. Can it really be true that cowboys would line up to help the

cook on the trail drive grind coffee, just hoping he would give them a little stick of peppermint candy that came with the coffee shipment? The idea of tough cowboys vying with one another to help "Coosie" (as they called their cooks) for a bit of candy seems silly and out of place.

So is the vision of Eskimos playing video games and watching MTV, living in prefab housing in the Arctic. It just does not fit with what "Eskimo" means. We are far more comfortable with snow igloos and whale blubber, harpoons and kayaks.

Although the cultures dealt with in Lucent's The Way People Live series are often historically and socially well known, the emphasis is on the personal aspects of life. Groups of people, while unquestionably affected by their politics and their governmental structures, are more than those institutions. How do people in a particular time and place educate their children? What do they eat? And how do they build their houses? What kinds of work do they do? What kinds of games do they enjoy? The answers to these questions bring these cultures to life. People's lives are revealed in the particulars and only by knowing the particulars can we understand these cultures' will to survive and their moments of weakness and greatness.

This is not to say that understanding politics does not help to understand a culture. There is no question that the Warsaw ghetto, for example, was a culture that was brought about by the politics and social ideas of Adolf

Hitler and the Third Reich. But the Jews who were crowded together in the ghetto cannot be understood by the Reich's politics. Their life was a day-to-day battle for existence, and the creativity and methods they used to prolong their lives is a vital story of human perseverance that would be denied by focusing only on the institutions of Hitler's Germany. Knowing that children as young as five or six outwitted Nazi guards on a daily basis, that Jewish policemen helped the Germans control the ghetto, that children attended secret schools in the ghetto and even earned diplomas—these are the things that reveal the fabric of life, that can inspire, intrigue, and amaze.

Books in The Way People Live series allow both the casual reader and the student to see humans as victims, heroes, and onlookers. And although humans act in ways that can fill us with feelings of sorrow and revulsion, it is important to remember that "hero," "predator," and "victim" are dangerous terms. Heaping undue pity or praise on people reduces them to objects, and strips them of their humanity.

Seeing the Jews of Warsaw only as victims is to deny their humanity. Seeing them only as they appear in surviving photos, staring at the camera with infinite sadness, is limiting, both to them and to those who want to understand them. To an object of pity, the only appropriate response becomes "Those poor creatures!" and that reduces both the quality of their struggle and the depth of their despair. No one is served by such two-dimensional views of people and their cultures.

With this in mind, The Way People Live series strives to flesh out the traditional, two-dimensional views of people in various cultures and historical circumstances. Using a wide variety of primary quotations—the words not only of the politicians and government leaders, but of the real people whose lives are being examined—each book in the series attempts to show an honest and complete picture of a culture removed from our own by time or space.

By examining cultures in this way, the reader will notice not only the glaring differences from his or her own culture, but also will be struck by the similarities. For indeed, people share common needs—warmth, good company, stability, and affirmation from others. Ultimately, seeing how people really live, or have lived, can only enrich our understanding of ourselves.

Black Blizzards

Sunday, April 14, 1935, began as a warm spring day in the western part of Oklahoma known as the Panhandle. The sun shone, birds sang, and a gentle southwest wind stirred the fields. In the small town of Guymon and in others like it, where most people were Protestant and went to church, people fanned themselves while ministers led them in prayers for rain. Severe drought—residents called it "drouth"—had plagued the Great Plains for five years, and crops were badly in need of moisture. "Good rains within three weeks mean a harvest," declared Reverend R.L. Wells at the Methodist Episcopal Church. "God rules all and our last resort is prayer."[1]

When services ended, people flocked outside, ready to take advantage of the good weather. Some went on picnics. Others visited neighbors or went home to plant their gardens. Before the afternoon was over, however, ominous changes occurred in the weather. In some places, the temperature dropped fifty degrees in a few hours. In others, the stillness caused birds to flutter and chatter nervously.

Then a huge cloud appeared on the horizon. Dark brown at the top, inky at the base, it towered at least a thousand feet high. "From the north, here it came," remembered Jerry Shannon, who lived in the small town of Felt, Oklahoma. "Just a whole boil, roll and boil."[2] As it rolled forward at a terrifying pace, thousands of excited wild geese, ducks, and smaller birds took to the air. Some people noticed rainbow colors dancing in the sky above the cloud. Others did not stop to admire its grandeur. Recognizing it as a "black blizzard"—a mammoth dust storm that would turn day to night and smother everything in its path—they raced for cover as fast as they could.

Many were not successful. Vesta Tuna of Texhoma, Oklahoma, was bringing in her cows when she was overtaken. She threw herself flat on the ground, covered her head with her apron, and struggled to breathe through dust so thick that it totally blocked the sun. Arthur N. Howe of Beaver County, Oklahoma, was feeding cattle when the wind and total darkness hit him. He took shelter against his wagon and huddled there while blowing sand scoured his skin and clothes.

Even those who were inside felt the swirling terror of the storm, which lasted three hours in some places. Lila Lee King and a friend were at home in Liberal, Kansas, that afternoon. She remembered, "I was sure I was going to die. . . . We lit matches and held them before our face and we couldn't see the light unless it was quite near."[3]

A Stricken Region

"Black Sunday," as April 14 would later be called, marked the most fearsome of hundreds of catastrophic dust storms that struck America's heartland between 1932 and 1938. In 1932, fourteen dust storms were reported, and in the following year, the number jumped to thirty-eight. A record twenty-three dust storms buffeted Oklahoma and neighboring states in May 1937 alone, and there were at least seventy-two for the year. Like the Black Sunday event, many storms began in the Dakotas and swept across Wyoming, eastern Colorado, and western Kansas, picking up dirt out of the dry fields and carrying it miles across the land.

Those who lived in the path of the storms were repeatedly battered by winds that could reach over seventy miles an hour. If outside, people gasped and choked. If inside, they watched the fine swirling soil seep through sealed doors and windows to coat furniture, dishes, clothes, and skin. After calm returned, dead rabbits and birds littered the fields. Crops lay flattened. Livestock were caked with dirt. People lay dead.

The area affected by these storms, including northeastern New Mexico, southeastern Colorado, western Kansas, and the panhandles of Texas and Oklahoma, became known as the "dust bowl." Montana, Nebraska, and North and South Dakota were involved to a lesser degree. The shape of the dust bowl changed annually depending on the amount of rain that fell in a particular area, but the worst wind erosion centered on Liberal, Kansas, and included a one-hundred-mile region around that town.

Despite its name, the dust bowl was not bowl shaped, nor was it an area of low elevation.

A dust storm engulfs an Oklahoma farm. During the 1930s, a series of such storms swept across the Great Plains, devastating an area that became known as the "dust bowl."

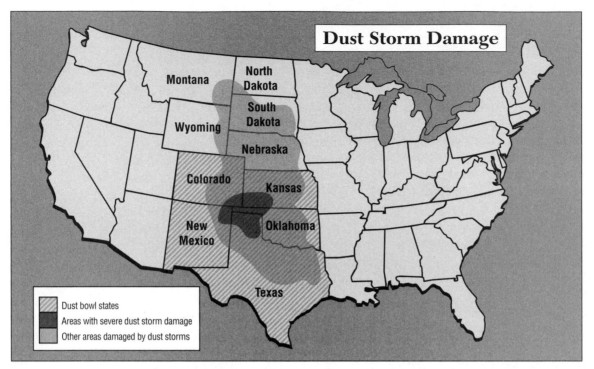

Dust Storm Damage

Montana
North Dakota
South Dakota
Wyoming
Nebraska
Colorado
Kansas
New Mexico
Oklahoma
Texas

Dust bowl states
Areas with severe dust storm damage
Other areas damaged by dust storms

In fact, it was part of the Great Plains, a vast, dry grass highland that stretches from northern Canada to southern Texas and from the Rocky Mountains eastward for about four hundred miles. The name "dust bowl" was casually coined by Associated Press reporter Robert E. Geiger, who was familiar with the Rose Bowl and Orange Bowl football championships. He used the term in one of a series of articles he wrote for the *Washington (D.C.) Evening Star* in April 1935. On April 15, he stated, "Three little words . . . rule life in the dust bowl of the continent—if it rains."[4]

Geiger never used the phrase "dust bowl" again, but it caught all America's attention. The term seemed to suit the situation in the nation's heartland, and it was used thereafter in letters, speeches, and other newspaper articles. For everyone who read it, it conjured up visions of poverty, drought, wind erosion, and terrible storms, all of which were a part of one of the most tragic periods in U.S. history.

"Awe Inspiring"

Although dirt began blowing in 1932, a dust storm that struck on the afternoon of January 21, 1933, in the Texas panhandle served as the unofficial beginning of the dust bowl. The event was not as frightening as the Black Sunday storm would be, but its destructiveness was a warning that trouble was on the way. Plate-glass windows were broken in Amarillo before the storm moved on into Oklahoma and Kansas. There it destroyed property and most of the wheat crop. The Amarillo weather bureau called the storm "most spectacular" and "awe inspiring."[5]

Everyone soon learned, however, that dust storms were to be dreaded rather than admired. Called "black blizzards," "dusters," "rollers," and "sand blows," they occurred each spring during the 1930s. Some struck in the fall as well. Some were relatively localized, such as a storm that enveloped just the state of Colorado on March 11, 1936, and continued for two days, reducing all visibility to less than a mile. Others blew over a hundred thousand square miles, carrying dust high into the sky and pushing it two to three thousand miles across the ground.

One storm that affected an enormous part of the United States began on May 9, 1934. On that day, a dust cloud that extended from the Canadian border to Oklahoma and covered fifteen hundred miles from the Rocky Mountains to the Great Lakes moved across country. By late afternoon, 12 million tons of dust from Montana and Wyoming was falling like snow over Chicago. Buffalo, New York, was darkened by dust in the middle of the next day, and on May 11, dust settled over Boston, New York City, Washington, D.C., and Atlanta, Georgia. The storm finally moved out to sea, where ships three hundred miles out found dust on their decks a day or two later.

There was no predicting a storm's size or power. The gale-force winds might last one hour or three days. They might be accompanied by thunder or be eerily quiet. The sand they carried might be red, brown, black, yellow, or gray, depending on its origin. People who experienced a number of blows claimed that different types of dirt had their own characteristic smell, from a sharp peppery nip to a nauseating greasiness.

Sometimes the storms were light enough that people carried on normal activities despite them. Most often, however, the blows were disruptive and dangerous. They tore off roofs, crushed homes, and killed people and animals. Coupled with heat and drought, they did severe damage to crops, in some cases wiping out thousands of acres of wheat, corn, or cotton in a single day. According to a federal government report, 35 million acres of cropland were destroyed and another 100 million acres were seriously damaged as early

"Are We in It?"

People talk about the dust bowl as though it encompassed a specific bowl-shaped region in the United States, but in fact the problem area moved and reshaped year to year, depending on the weather. Historian Donald Worster explains in his book *Dust Bowl: The Southern Plains in the 1930s.*

"In 1935 the Dust Bowl reached well down into the cotton belt of west Texas, but three years later it had moved northeastward, making Kansas the most extensively affected state. By 1939 the serious blow area within the Bowl had shrunk to about one-fifth its original size: it increased again to 22 million acres in 1940, then in the forties it disappeared.

The difficulty in making the Dust Bowl . . . fixed and precise was that it roamed around a good deal—it was an event as well as a locality. A puzzled tourist stopped George Taton, a Kansas wheat farmer, in Garden City one day: 'Can you tell me where this Dust Bowl is?' 'Stay where you are,' Taton told him, 'and it'll come to you.' Even locals could not always discover the exact boundaries, wondering exasperatedly, 'Are we in it or ain't we?' In a sense, wherever there were recurring dust storms and soil erosion there was a dust bowl, and by that test most of the Great Plains was 'in it' during a part of the 1930s, some of the most severe conditions occurring as far north as Nebraska and the Dakotas."

as 1934. Wheat yields declined from an average of twenty-seven bushels per acre in the late 1920s to less than three bushels per acre in 1937. For farmers already suffering economic hardships during the Great Depression, the loss of income was devastating.

Setting the Stage for Tragedy

The story of life in the dust bowl is about those farmers and others who struggled to survive during a decade of drought, depression, and storms that were larger than life. As Kansas resident Avis D. Carlson wrote in a *New Republic* article in 1935, "We live with the dust, eat it, sleep with it, watch it strip us of possessions and the hope of possessions."[6]

Some people gave up the struggle and left the region to look for a better life. The majority, however, stayed on their land, worked, raised their children, and waited for better times to return. Their persistence, industriousness, optimism, and humor carried them through. "We've got the greatest country in the world if we can just get a few kinks straightened out," declared John L. McCarty, editor of the *Dalhart Texan*. "Let's keep boosting [improving] our country."[7]

Ironically, it was enthusiasm and a strong work ethic that first led Americans to plow up the plains, setting the stage for the dusty tragedy that struck in the 1930s. As historian Donald Worster writes, "By the values they had been taught, they were justified in what they did; they were contributors, they assumed, to national growth and affluence."[8] Little did they realize that their industriousness would lead to acres of shifting sand and that, in spite of their hard work, they would live with hard times for decades to come.

CHAPTER 1

The Great Plow-Up

The dust bowl was one of the darkest periods of life on America's Great Plains. During that time, a combination of environmental and human-made conditions created a natural crisis unseen before in the twentieth century. Author T.H. Watkins describes the process:

> The land had been broken and exposed by repeated plowing, leached of its nutrients by constant planting and replanting, grazed down to the dirt by cattle and sheep, its topsoil skinned off in sheets or gullied by water erosion during wet years. And it was on these lands that the sun had been doing some of its most devastating work during the drought years.[9]

Dry and Dusty History

People had to be tough to live on the Great Plains, and those who did could testify that drought, wind, and blowing dust were common to the region. In 1830, Baptist missionary Isaac McCoy recorded being caught in two dust storms while surveying parts of eastern Kansas. One of these storms mixed dust with ashes from a recent prairie fire, making it impossible for McCoy to see much past his horse's head. "The dust, sand, and ashes were so dense that one appeared in danger of suffocation,"[10] he wrote.

In the 1850s, newspaper editors in Kansas Territory wrote about winds and blowing dirt. One editor noted,

> We are frank to confess that we have felt more inconvenience from the wind and dust, since our arrival in Kansas, than from any other source. Our houses are all open, and the wind whistles in at every crevice, bringing along with it a heavy load of fine particles of charcoal, ashes, etc., and depositing it on our type, paper, library, furniture, and in fact not regarding our dinner, but liberally covering it with condiment for which we have no relish [11]

Dust storms were so bad in 1880 that the *Wichita Eagle* carried the following complaint: "Dust, grit, and sand everywhere—in your victuals [food], up your nose, down your back, between your toes. . . . Out of doors people communicate by signs. When they would talk they must retire to some room without windows or a crack, pull out their ear plugs and wash their mouths."[12]

Such storms stemmed in part from the climate of the region. Although it could be pleasantly breezy and sun-swept, it was also subject to extremes of hot and cold, wet and dry. In winter, blizzards lashed the plains, and alternate periods of freezing and thawing loosened the ground and made it prone to erosion. Summer temperatures rose above one hundred degrees with low humidity, evaporating the little rain that fell and leaving everything bone-dry. Strong winds that blew every spring and summer added to the dry atmosphere. When rain was adequate, plants grew well, but mild droughts every three to four years made early settlers turn to ranching rather than farming. More severe droughts, which occurred about every twenty years, dried the grasslands and put a strain even on ranchers.

Tough native plants such as buffalo grass were well suited to grow on the plains. Surviving on little water, these plants held the soil together with their deep roots, creating a mat called sod. Sod was so thick and tough that early settlers often cut it into chunks and used it to build homes. Prairie grass made the soil largely impervious to wind, but prairie fires and overgrazing by herds of cattle bared the soil and exposed it to the elements. When so exposed, dirt blew easily in even the lightest breeze. Because the soil was composed of fine particles that did not easily clump once

An Oklahoma farmer and his two sons run to their small farmhouse to take cover from a dust storm.

they became dry, it allowed even small amounts of rain to quickly drain or evaporate away.

Settling the Plains

Weather and soil quality contributed to blowing dust on the plains, but farm practices were the key that sparked disaster in the 1930s. Americans began farming the plains in the 1800s, but emphasis was placed on raising livestock rather than crops. Herds of cattle and sheep were introduced, and they thrived on native plant vegetation, which usually proved adequate to their needs.

In 1862, the government began encouraging people to settle the plains. The Homestead Act of that year allowed settlers to claim 160 acres of land and receive free title to it if they cultivated and made improvements on at least a part of it. In 1873, the Timber Culture Act allowed settlers to claim 160 acres of land if they agreed to plant 40 acres of trees. In 1877, the Desert Land Act allowed settlers to claim 640 acres of land provided they agreed to irrigate it. Author Pamela Riney-Kehrberg says,

> You had railroad companies and states putting out advertisements encouraging people to think of this land as a bountiful land. The State of Kansas put out posters showing watermelons the size of . . . small automobiles, grapes the size of bowling balls, corn that you had to pick by going up a ladder, and people were encouraged to believe that this was the Garden of Eden if they would only have the courage to go out and challenge the land.[13]

As a result, families looking for land settled in the area. They set up small homesteads where they could be independent and self-sufficient,

Everlasting Wind

In his book *The Dust Bowl: An Agricultural and Social History*, Douglas Hurt points out that the Great Plains have a history of winds and dust that dates back to early times. The April 15, 1880, edition of the *Wichita Eagle*, in which the editor complains of conditions prevailing in Kansas that year, proves his point.

"It may be asserted here and now that Kansas as a paradise has her failings, not the least of which is her everlasting spring winds. If there is a man, woman or child in Sedgwick County whose eyes are not filled with dust and their minds with disgust, he, she, or it must be an idiot or awful pious. From everlasting to everlasting this wind for a week has just sat down on its hind legs and howled and screeched and snorted until you couldn't tell your grandfather from a jackass rabbit. And its sand backs up its blow with oceans of grit to spare. We saw a preacher standing on the corner the other day with his back up, his coattails over his head, and his chapeau [hat] sailing heavenward, spitting mud out of his mouth and looking unutterable things. He dug the sand out of his eyes and the gravel out of his hair, and said nothing. It wouldn't have been right. But we know what he thought."

and they began working the land. The process involved long hours of backbreaking labor, including walking behind a horse and plow, sowing seed by hand, hoeing weeds, and bringing in crops, but most settlers were used to hard work and sacrifice.

As time passed, improvements in farm implements made cultivating the plains easier. The most significant advance was the

Modern Methods

Farm equipment was becoming modern by the 1920s, and residents of the Great Plains were impressed. In R. Douglas Hurt's book *The Dust Bowl: An Agricultural and Social History*, a newspaper reporter in the Oklahoma panhandle expresses his admiration for advances that allowed a bountiful harvest with less work.

"Occasionally we would run across a field where the old binders [machines that tie grain into bundles] were being used, and the great number of shocks [stacks] would attest the splendid production and the belief of some of the farmers that the old shocked and threshed wheat pans out best. . . .

But when one sees a combine and tractor manned by one person sitting in the shade of a large umbrella, cutting a swath of wheat twenty feet wide, and not shaking down so much of the grain as the old ten-foot harvester did, and the clean grain falling into the wagon bed alongside the combine, as compared with the header driver, four barge men and two stackers not to mention the threshing crew . . . one realizes its advantage, and the labor expense saved. A marvelous number of new auto trucks swept by us, and they carried loads both to and from the market. Going in they were loaded with wheat, and coming back they were loaded with new disc plows and machinery to be used in following the combines and headers in preparing the land for next year's crops."

Modern farm equipment like this gas-powered tractor and combine harvester helped farmers produce a bountiful harvest with very little work.

development of gasoline-powered tractors and combines—machines that cut and threshed grain in a single operation. Both made plowing, planting, and harvesting quicker and easier.

Quickly recognizing the profits to be gained from buying these machines, farmers bought them as soon as they could afford them. Ownership went from less than three hundred tractors in southwestern Kansas in 1915 to over three thousand in 1925. Enthusiasm for the new machines was expressed by one Meade County, Kansas, farmer who, with the help of a hired man, plowed around the clock in certain seasons. He wrote, "My tractor roared day and night, and I was turning eighty acres every twenty-four hours, only stopping for servicing once every six hours."[14]

With easier methods to plow up prairie sod, productivity increased. In 1910, farmers harvested 970,000 acres of corn, oats, wheat, barley, rye, and sorghum in a twenty-seven-county area. In 1920, acreage for these crops totaled over 2 million acres. But now, not only was there less grass to hold down the soil, the constant cultivation necessary to grow crops set the stage for new problems.

Erroneous Practices

Most farmers were ignorant of soil conservation and erosion control practices in the early 1900s. They knew that the plains were subject to droughts, but they focused on the present and assumed they would be able to make it through the dry periods if they had to. "Most of the people living in the area were pretty well caught up in the dream of progress and turning this place into a bread basket. So if there were misgivings, they were not being published. . . . There was an enormous sense of invulnerability [security], at least in official circles, and I think to a large extent among

settlers and farmers,"[15] remembers historian Donald Worster.

Some people did care about soil and water conservation, but many of them held the erroneous belief that the more intensely fields were cultivated, the better farming conditions would be. For instance, Hardy Webster Campbell, the father of "scientific dry land farming," stated in the 1880s that evaporation could be reduced and drifting soil made almost stationary by "dust mulching"— working the soil until a layer of fine particles lay on the surface. This layer supposedly provided insulation against drying. Campbell also believed that all organic material should be eliminated during the fallow season. Bare land did not have plants that sapped its moisture. "The real difficulty in the semi-arid belt is not a lack of rainfall, but the loss of too much by evaporation, and this can be largely controlled by proper cultivation,"[16] Campbell stated. Most of his methods, however, allowed more evaporation and wind erosion rather than less.

In general, farmers plowed, planted, and harvested with little thought of the bad effect they had on the land. "[The plows] just scratched the top of the soil," remembers Ronald Fronk, who lived in Beaver County, Oklahoma. "It made the soil into powder."[17] To prepare their fields for next year's harvest, they burned off the crop stubble, effectively removing organic matter that would have held the soil down. Those who raised cattle also allowed the animals to graze until grass was extremely short or even killed off entirely.

The Crop of Choice

Until about 1920, rain was adequate to support careless practices on the Great Plains.

During World War I, the government encouraged Great Plains farmers to grow wheat to help satisfy overseas demand for the grain.

Landowners planted crops for which there was much demand, such as wheat, barley, rye, and corn. Cotton was also popular in some areas. Good harvests and high crop prices made farming seem almost too profitable to be true. Stories ran in eastern newspapers of homesteaders who had made their fortunes in just a few years. One article stated: "[An Ohio stonemason] arrived . . . with a large family and very little money. He took up a homestead claim. He began raising wheat. Last year, his daughter was married and as a wedding present he gave her a ten-thousand-dollar farm. He is worth not less than fifty thousand dollars."[18]

Wheat was the preferred crop for many farmers, especially when World War I broke out in Europe in 1914. The demand for grain overseas was high, and prices rose from less than a dollar a bushel to over two dollars a bushel in 1917. Government slogans such as "Wheat for the British!" and "Wheat will win the war!" encouraged more planting. "The forces that fight for freedom . . . depend upon us in an extraordinary and unexpected degree for sustenance, for supply of the materials by which men are to live and fight,"[19] pointed out President Woodrow Wilson in a special message to farmers. People who had land and did not plant wheat were labeled unpatriotic, so most farmers responded to the call without considering that they were relying on one crop alone to provide their livelihoods.

Not everyone believed that such a narrow focus was sensible. "Wisely or otherwisely, this region has permitted wheat growing to become its main concern,"[20] said author Caroline A. Henderson, a farm wife from Eva, Oklahoma. Henderson's point of view was largely ignored, however, even when the war was over and European farmers began producing their own wheat again. As prices fell, farmers on the plains simply plowed under more prairie land and planted more wheat in order to keep their incomes high. And, to get the work done quickly, some of them bought better tractors, larger combines, and trucks to carry their crops to market. All buying was done on credit, but it seemed worth the outlay, since the machines could be easily paid for when the crops were sold in the fall.

Turning the plains into wheat fields became known as "the great plow-up." Between 1910 and 1920, the area plowed totaled over 5 million acres, an area six times the size of the state of Delaware. Although some people wondered if agricultural good times could last forever, most shrugged the thought aside. Somehow the rains would continue, the weather would cooperate, and the demand for wheat would remain high. "I think we should prepare to grow more wheat and less kafir [corn]," opined C.W. Maxey of the *Oklahoma Farmer-Stockman* in 1921. "These western plains are proving to be well adapted to wheat and failure seldom occurs where proper methods are employed. Wheat is the universal bread grain of the whole world and indications are that there will not be any too much wheat grown for years to come."[21]

Suitcase Farmers

With farming so profitable, more and more people wanted to get into the business in a big way. Not only did farmers buy more land, taking out mortgages on land they already owned to pay for it, but others who were interested in making their fortunes began buying land as well. Many of these profiteers were police officers, dentists, business owners, and even criminals from urban areas like Kansas City, Chicago, New York, and Seattle. These people knew little about farming and did not care to learn. Locals called them "suitcase farmers."

After investing in the right machinery and using their vacation time to get a wheat crop

"We Don't Think"

As Texan Melt White observes in "*Surviving the Dust Bowl*" on the PBS website (www. pbs.org), the destruction of the plains in the 1930s resulted partly from people's failure to think about the future.

"That's kindly [kind of] a human trait: we don't think. We don't think, except for ourselves and it comes down to greed. You know, we're selfish and we want—we're self-centered and we want what we want and we don't even think of what the end results might be. Or, like a lot of people say, as far as you can see is the end of your nose and that's what a lot of people back then, they could just see the great thing that was happening, [what] the rain and the produce of the crops is doin'. So that's—that's about as far as they see and that's as far as they thought. They didn't think in the future what could happen if things did change."

in the ground, suitcase farmers usually returned to their homes in the city, leaving the crops to grow until the time was right to harvest them. These city people cared nothing about the land. Profits were the key, and if conditions were right and the crop was good, they made a great deal of money. If things went wrong, they sold out or abandoned their fields, none the worse because they still had their jobs in the city. "People came in and broke up this land to plant wheat," remembered Grace McKinnis, who lived in Springfield, Colorado, for most of her ninety years. "They broke up the land, and then we didn't have rain. And they just left it."[22]

One of the most well known of the suitcase farmers was Hickman Price, also known as the wheat king because of the size of his farming operation. Price moved to Plainview, Texas, in 1929 after quitting his job as a motion picture executive in New York. He bought and leased 34,500 acres of land—almost fifty-four square miles—near Plainview and hired wheat farmers from Minnesota, Nebraska, and the Dakotas to oversee his operations. He ordered a large number of trucks, tractors, plows, combines, and other farming equipment, set up shops where repairs could be made, and set his men to plowing and planting day and night, winter and summer. Twenty-five combines were required to bring in the wheat at harvest time. Newspapers around the country called him "the world's largest individual wheat farmer,"[23] and a delegation from the Union of Soviet Socialist Republics came to Texas to study his methods.

Debt, Disaster, and the Great Depression

Although the 1920s were prosperous times for some American wheat farmers like Price,
the many small farmers of the Great Plains did not do as well. Elizabeth Day remembered her years on a farm in Nebraska:

> It was always too hot, too cold, too dry . . . insects and locusts. . . . There was hail, of course, which often stripped the wheat or corn. When it was time to harvest the wheat it was always with an eye on the sky to hurry and get it in before the rains came, or the hail, or something to ruin the crop. It was almost as if the cosmos was trying to kick us out of the area.[24]

The price of most farm products was low throughout the decade, and many farmers who had mortgages lost their farms because they could not pay for them. Many banks in farm areas failed during the decade, reducing the opportunities for new loans and sometimes taking farmers' hard-earned savings down with them.

Farm problems were compounded when the stock market crashed in late 1929, sweeping the entire nation into the Great Depression. On October 24, more than 12 million shares of stock were traded on the New York Stock Exchange, and investors lost $4 billion. Five days later, the market lost billions more. Suddenly, the national economy was on shaky ground. Everyone's savings were gone. Businesses failed and millions of Americans—up to one-fourth of the labor force—were put out of work. "Almost overnight it was like a bomb had fallen,"[25] remembered one woman.

The effect on already struggling farmers was disastrous. Wheat prices dropped dramatically. Farmers responded by plowing up more land and planting more wheat. This time that remedy did not work. By late summer, the price of wheat had fallen from $1.60 to less than twenty-five cents a bushel and farmers could not sell enough to recover their costs and pay their debts. Relying on their livestock did not solve the problem either. The price of beef and hogs dropped dramatically; farmers received less than half as much for an animal in 1934 as they had in 1929.

Not only were prices low and debts being called in by banks that were on the verge of failure, but the weather turned extremely dry as well. In 1931 and 1932, Hickman Price and thousands of others watched their crops shrivel and die. Instead of harvesting five hundred thousand bushels of wheat, the wheat king harvested thirty-three thousand.

Instead of getting two dollars a bushel, he got thirty-five cents.

"It Was Unreal"

With prices low, money tight, and drought affecting more than half of the nation, all it took was one more factor—wind—to create disaster on the plains. Year after year between 1932 and 1938, the wind churned across dry fields, creating dust storms that

Panicked traders crowd the sidewalks outside the New York Stock Exchange following the stock market crash of 1929.

sheared off grass at the roots, dug craters around fence posts, and made mountains out of once flat fields. As historian Vance Johnson writes, "Every wind was destructive, and the wind blew almost every day. . . . Acre by acre, the crops were torn out by their roots and carried away."[26] In 1935 alone, 850 million tons of topsoil "so rich," an observer noted, that it "looked like chocolate where the plow turned the sod"[27] blew away from over 4 million acres on the plains. With the topsoil went nutrients and organic material, leaving behind a sterile hardpan soil that was as hard as cement.

When the dust blew, every aspect of daily life was affected and even the most courageous and determined pioneers had to call on reserves of strength they had never tapped before. To make matters worse, no one knew how long the drought would last. No one knew if the rain would come next year. No one knew if they would be able to survive another year if it did not. All anybody could do was fight the dust and try to go on with their lives. Melt White, son of a Texas farmer, said:

My mother . . . she'd be walkin' the floor . . . and she'd wring her hands and say, "Oh, the wind, the wind, the wind." And she'd just cry, because she realized the conditions things was in. I didn't. I just thought, "Well, it's dry and the wind's blowin' and the sand's blowin'." But she realized how Dad was havin' to work, what little he was makin', and we'as about to starve to death.[28]

Life in the Dusters

When the wind blew in the dust bowl, something as ordinary as breathing became a challenge. Imogene Glover remembered, "When those dust storms blew and you were out in 'em, it would just coat the inside of your nose literally. And sometimes your mouth would just get cottony dry because, well, you spit out dirt sometimes. It looked like tobacco juice, only it was dirt, when you'd spit. It was pretty awful. But I just thought that was part of livin'. Everybody else was in the same boat."[29]

The blowing dirt made daily routines burdensome and depressing. Whether one was trying to keep house, run a small business, go to school, or go to church, one had to fight the weather. In cities and towns, the impact of the dust was serious. Rural families had it worse, as North Dakota native Ann Marie Low explained, "As far as one can see are brown pastures and fields which, in the wind, just rise up and fill the air with dirt. It tortures animals and humans, makes housekeeping an everlasting drudgery, and ruins machinery. . . . Trees are dying by the thousands. Cattle and horses are dying, some from starvation and some from the dirt they eat on the grass."[30]

Ever-Present Dust

Ann Marie Low, a teenager in the 1930s, could testify that wind and dust were extremely frustrating for farm women, for whom the chores of housekeeping and cooking were all-important. Being known as a good housekeeper or a good cook was as important as being a patriot and a churchgoer.

Although farm women took pride in well-scrubbed floors and a clean parlor, maintaining such conditions during storms was impossible. Everything that had a surface became dusty. Clothes hanging on the line to dry ended up stiff with dirt. Families went to sleep on clean sheets and pillowcases and awoke to find everything dirty but the spots where they had lain.

Dust settled on furniture, piled on window ledges, and trickled down walls like tiny waterfalls. It seeped into closets and lay in ripples across floors. Ann Marie Low wrote in her diary, "I'm writing this lying on the living room floor, dripping sweat and watching the dirt drift in the windows and across the floor. I've dusted this whole house twice today and won't do it again."[31]

Pictures hanging on wires became heavy with dust and fell to the floor. So much dust piled up in attics that some homes collapsed on their owners. Imogene Glover of Oklahoma remembered,

One night when I was sleeping in a little room, my mother and dad were in the big room with my baby sister in bed. And the ceiling started falling in with the dust so heavy on it. . . . They got out okay, 'cause Daddy yelled at Mother. He could hear it comin' down and he said, "Grab that kid, Mom." . . . They all got outside as soon as they knew that the ceiling was fallin' in as a result of the dust sifting in.[32]

Many women delayed housecleaning during storms, although some cleaning was necessary so that vital activities like eating and sleeping could continue. Most women tried to minimize the dust by sealing every crack through which it could enter the house. Because many homes were poorly constructed and poorly insulated, this could be a big job. Tape or putty was usually applied around windows, doors, and other gaps, while wet cloths were stuffed in larger spaces to shut off drafts. Some women became so skilled at this job that there was little air circulation inside. Kerosene lanterns flickered from lack of oxygen when a family was cooped up for several hours.

Despite the sealing process, dust still managed to seep inside, where the smell permeated everything and lingered even after a good scrubbing. During the worst storms, people had trouble seeing each other across rooms. A woman from Garden City, Kansas, said, "All we could do about it was just sit in our dusty chairs, gaze at each other through the fog that filled the room and watch that fog settle slowly and silently, covering everything—including ourselves—in a thick, brownish gray blanket. . . . The door and windows were all shut tightly, yet those tiny particles seem to seep through the very walls."[33]

Grit in the Teeth

During ordinary times, most farm women took great pride in their cooking, as Low noted in her diary: "The meals were lavish. A farm wife would have disgraced herself and her husband if she had not prepared a good

Cattle carcasses rot in the sun following a severe dust storm. Livestock in the dust bowl often died of starvation or suffocation.

meal—platters of fried chicken as well as either a beef or pot roast, heaping bowls of mashed potatoes, several kinds of vegetables from her garden, homemade bread or rolls, butter, jelly and jam, pickles, pies, and cake."[34] But meals were not always so lavish during the hard days of the 1930s. Money was spent on staples such as flour, sugar, and coffee, and those supplies were used carefully. Many families grew used to eating the same thing repeatedly, such as biscuits or produce from the garden. Oklahoman Juanita Price described her experiences: "I can remember . . . in summer we were eating string beans and corn. My father finally got a little job that would pay him $24 a month, and that was to feed himself, my mother, and eight children."[35]

Even the best cook found it hard to provide an appetizing meal during a dust storm. In the kitchen, surfaces and utensils had to be washed and wiped before they could be used. Low remembered, "Before starting breakfast I had to sweep and wash all the dirt off the kitchen and dining room floors, wash the stove, pancake griddle, and dining room table and chairs."[36] Because dust filtered into cupboards, they had to be wiped out before clean dishes were put inside, and women kept glasses and cups always turned upside down. Plates were washed after meals and again just before it was time to put food in them again.

Women learned to mix bread dough inside a drawer with a towel over their hands and arms in order to keep it free from grit. Milk was covered as soon as it came out of the cow and then sealed into glass mason jars so that it would not turn to sludge. To drink the milk, people punched holes in the lids and inserted straws. Meats were baked rather than fried, because ovens sealed out most dirt particles. Anything that was fried was cooked over very high heat so the air rising above would lift the dust away.

Dust Bowl Blues

Even after people knew how to prepare for a dust storm, its arrival did not get any easier. In T.H. Watkins's, *The Hungry Years: A Narrative History of the Great Depression in America*, one woman describes her feelings and her preparations as she catches sight of the familiar cloud on the horizon.

"My heart seemed to leap into my throat; I felt sick and weak. . . . I went back into the house, hastily covered the table with newspapers and an old cloth, covered the water pail, covered all the unwashed cooking utensils, made my bed and spread an old denim comforter over it. . . . Next I put on an old stocking cap to protect my hair, an old jacket to comfort my shaking body, and sat down by the kitchen range with my feet on the oven door.

The room soon filled with a dust haze through which the coal-oil lamp made a pale light, and for the first and only time during the dust storms I abandoned myself to an orgy of [uncontrolled] weeping."

Eating itself was a challenge during a storm. Everyone ate immediately when the food came to the table, but even then it was gritty with dust. Some families gave up their manners and ate out of the pot on the stove. One farm wife near Griggs, Oklahoma, placed everything on the table under a tablecloth and then told her family to duck underneath the cloth to eat. Dirt was minimized, but according to her husband, "it was extremely difficult to pass the food or train the children in good table manners"[37] using this approach.

A young girl stands in the kitchen of her family's farmhouse. Maintaining a clean kitchen in the dust bowl was virtually impossible.

Deadly Wind

There was no minimizing dirt outdoors on a farm, so everyone performed the multitude of tasks—plowing and planting, feeding and caring for animals, milking cows and feeding chickens—in the dust unless storms became too thick and smothering. Many families strung guide ropes or wires from the house to the barn so they could make their way back and forth without getting lost.

The safety of farm animals was of high importance, and at the first sign of a coming storm, all were brought into shelter if possible. If left outside, chickens and turkeys suffocated in the dust. Other animals wandered away over the tops of buried fences and were lost. "In a rising sand storm, cattle quickly become blinded," observed photojournalist Margaret Bourke-White. "They run around in circles until they fall and breathe so much dust that they die. Autopsies show their lungs caked with dust and mud."[38] Horses and mules also became agitated when they could not breathe, so some farmers covered their eyes and muzzles with gunnysacks to keep them comfortable. Pregnant animals also had to be watched carefully, because newborns died within a few hours if not carried in out of a storm.

Unlike farm animals, crops could not be saved when a storm struck. Those that were not blown flat were dried to a crisp by the wind that hissed over them. "Our cotton would be about five or six inches tall and it looked like a fire had gone over that field of cotton. It would just kill it. . . . The leaves would all be dead because it would just blacken it,"[39] remembered Vera Criswell of Baylor County, Texas.

Once destroyed, plants were torn out by the roots and carried away by the wind, which first blew the topsoil away and then carved craters four or five feet deep. In places, hardpan soil deep below the surface was exposed, while in others, outbuildings, gardens, and homes were half buried in huge drifts of dirt. Journalist Michael Parfit describes the contrast: "Fences would be buried to the top wire, and next to them yucca plants, called soapweed, would stand nakedly on stilts of their roots."[40]

Fighting the Dust

Despite the impact that storms had on outdoor activities, men determinedly worked their fields in all but the worst conditions. Crops were their livelihood and losing them meant destitution, so seeds were planted even if most of them blew out of the furrow or dried up in the heat. When the wind blew, farmers rode their tractors wearing goggles to protect their eyes and handkerchiefs across their nose and mouth. One traveler noted their stamina with amazement. "Over this high, parched region of gray, interminable plain a wind blows hot and dirty with a peculiar low, roaring resonance from the south. . . . Out in this blast of dust, bitten by it, hidden by it, their denims, their hands and faces matted with the grime of it, the men of West Kansas whistle, and go right on sowing wheat."[41]

Men were driven inside only when the wind was strongest. Elbert Mendenhall of Ponca, Nebraska, remembered the Fourth of July in 1936 when the wind was blowing "tornado strength":

Just steady wind at 116 degrees—just like blowing out of an oven. The leaves on the trees—it was dry anyhow, not much moisture in the soil—the leaves on the trees all curled up to protect themselves. . . . Corn just stood up there like a pinnacle—curled up. . . . I came in at noon and said, "I'm not going back out there with the wind blowing like that if I starve to

A large sand drift buries a dust bowl farm. Dust storms often generated huge drifts of dirt that buried entire buildings.

death—ain't no sense in it." I just . . . laid down in the dining room and went to sleep.[42]

Farmers who were caught in the fields during the black blizzards had to use their ingenuity to survive. Some followed a fence wire that they knew would lead them home. Others crawled on their hands and knees down furrows until they reached the shelter of their truck.

During storms, farm tools found new uses when families retreated to their cellars. Imogene Glover recalled,

My daddy took the hoe and ax and a scoop to the cellar with us and I know that he took the ax in case it covered up the door and he had to break the wood in the cellar door to get us out. Then he needed the scoop to scoop the dirt out. The only reason I think that he took the hoe was because it had the longest handle and he could poke it up through the vent in the ceiling of the cellar to be sure that we were getting air and didn't cover up that hole where our air vent was.[43]

Uncommon Bravery

In order to make a living, farmers worked their fields even though the wind blew at gale strength. As Vance Johnson writes in his book *Heaven's Tableland: The Dust Bowl Story*, it was often a punishing task, but they continued day after day.

"It was hard enough for a man to keep up with his own blowing [land]. If he had three fields to plow, the first was likely to be blowing again by the time he had finished the third. Blowing had become contagious. A man could do a perfect job of working his own land, but if his neighbor's fields were left untended they moved over on him and his own land began to blow more than ever. . . .

It took all the gumption a man had to stay astride his tractor seat through a full day. Dirt filled his eyes and his nostrils. The wind whistled so loudly about his ears that sometimes the roaring tractor exhaust dwindled away to a distant hum. After several hours his vision became distorted and everything about him seemed vague and unreal. Time lost its meaning."

Dust Sales and Saturday Matinees

While farm families suffered intensely during the storms, conditions were less severe in towns where buildings and trees served as windbreaks. There, homes were often more substantial, too, and close neighbors and friends could provide aid and moral support.

Townspeople found that movie theaters were particularly comfortable places to sit out a storm, because they were well built and even air-conditioned. In fact, patrons in one town who sat through a matinee on Black Sunday stepped outside after the storm had passed and wondered at the dark sky and the thick dirt that covered everything. Historian Vance Johnson notes, "Passersby told them what had happened. They could not believe what they heard."[44]

The dust and dirt had an impact on townspeople, however, even if it was not as menacing for them as for farmers. When black blizzards rolled in, all business and social activities ended. Communication lines blew down. People on the streets became disoriented and could not find their way to shelter. One woman who was visiting her sis-

A Place of Refuge

Being in town, close to people and other services, was comforting to farm families, but did not completely eliminate the hazards brought on by dust storms. In "Surviving the Dust Bowl" on the PBS website (www.pbs.org), Imogene Glover remembers conditions in Texoma, Oklahoma, in 1933.

"To begin with, we just had the low dust blowing off of the fields and my mother was expecting my . . . sister in 1933, and she said, 'We've got to get to town and stay in town, because a dust storm might come.' And she couldn't breathe good because she was expecting and she wanted to be where there were people. So we went into Tex-

oma for one month in July of '33. And we had low dust storms then. What I mean is you could still see the tops of the telephones poles. One of [the] . . . ladies from [the nearby town of] Gyman that had just started teaching at that time taught out at the Bethel School and she said that one started blowing before she could get to town and she couldn't see the road at all, but she could see the tops of the telephone poles and she drove by the telephone poles and right before she got into Gyman, the road turned, but the telephones didn't and she just followed the telephone poles on into town, cause she knew that they went to a building in town. And she followed them until she got there."

ter tried to walk back to her rooming house one block away and became confused and lost because she could see no landmarks. A passerby found her and guided her to the place, just across the street from where she was standing. "Lady Godiva could ride through the streets without even the horse seeing her,"[45] a journalist observed, referring to the English noblewoman who rode naked through the town of Coventry in the year 1040 to protest unfair taxation of her people.

The dust found its way into every building, from butcher shops to dentists' offices to watch repair shops. Clothing stores were hard-hit: many of their garments got soiled hanging on the rack. Historian Donald Worster reports that "in Dodge City a men's clothing store advertised a 'dust sale,' knocking shirts down to 75 cents."[46] In hospitals, the staff placed wet sheets over patients and struggled to maintain sterile conditions. In the Texas state legislature buildings in Austin,

senators wore surgical masks to breathe more easily.

Schoolchildren walked backwards to school to protect their faces from the stinging dust. Once in the school building, they were taught emergency procedures to follow when severe storms hit unexpectedly. "While I was in school," Imogene Glover recalled, "we had an old building that was two-stories and the teachers would tell us when these dust storms were rolling in to go to the hall and get under the stairs so that if the building blew away or blew down, we would be protected by the stairway. And this is how we went to school."[47]

In some towns, local business owners escorted schoolchildren home during blinding storms so they would not get lost. In other places, schools closed altogether in the spring when storms were worst. The risk of children getting lost or injured on their way to and from home was too great.

Travelers, Beware

Leaving shelter during a storm was always dangerous, even if one relied on the protection afforded by an automobile. With so much dust in the air, it was impossible to see more than a few feet in any direction, so drivers could easily run off the road. Some drivers missed curves and crashed. Others plowed into the back of trucks and were killed. In at least one town, police blocked highways and stopped motorists from traveling until the storm passed.

For those on foot, the risk of disaster was even greater. Several children got caught away from home when a storm hit; one was later found smothered to death, the other became tangled in barbed wire and barely managed to survive. A farmer on the road when a storm hit left his car and tried to walk the two miles to his home. He was found the next day suffocated to death.

The danger of being hit by stones and other debris that the wind picked up was high, too. One traveler, Philip Long, noticed that the air was full of blowing thistles on a day that he came upon a battered car that was pulled to the side of the road. Its windshield was gone and he assumed it was deserted until he looked inside and saw a man, a woman, and several children huddled on the seats. "I looked closer and gasped in amazement for those faces looked like porcupines. Their faces were driven so full of briars from the

A thick layer of sand covers a Colorado highway following a dust storm. Travel within the dust bowl was often very dangerous.

whistling thistles that they all, even the little ones, looked like they had a week's growth of whiskers. How they must have suffered before they were forced to stop."[48]

Heavy dust storms even halted public transportation systems. On March 26, 1935, a freight train near Dighton, Kansas, rammed a passenger train because the engineer could not see a warning signal through the blowing dirt. On January 18, 1938, a train was stalled for eighteen hours near Sublette, Kansas, because of dust drifts covering the tracks. Between Dodge City and Boise City, Oklahoma, workers for the Santa Fe Railroad had to use snowplows to remove dust from the tracks twice a week because of storms. One drift extended twenty-five hundred feet and averaged four feet deep.

Many people did not use their cars during dust storms for fear of ruining the engines. Even leaving vehicles sitting outside in a storm could be damaging, however. Pitted windshields and scoured-off paint testified to the abrasiveness of the dust. Helen Watson recalled the time in Nebraska when the family auto merely sat outside during a storm and got so much dirt in the motor that on Sunday morning when her husband started the car, dust blew out in a cloud and the family had to go back into the house to change clothing before they could go to church.

Static electricity, created by the dust particles rubbing together during storms, often caused automobile ignition systems to fail and cars to stall. Motorists learned to attach a drag wire and chains to their autos in order to ground the electricity and prevent the stalling problem.

Cars were not the only items to be affected by the static electricity, however. Wind-mills, pump handles, frying pans, and anything else made of metal could deliver a painful shock to anyone unwise enough to touch them during a storm.

Strong and Hopeful

Whether in towns, in the country, or on the road, conditions during dust storms had a nightmarish quality. Those who never experienced them were inclined to think the accounts they read were tall tales—exaggerations of the truth—because no weather event in modern history had ever been so prolonged, dramatic, and destructive. Those who witnessed the storms' power and ferocity, however, could testify that some of these were fearsome scourges, capable of making brave people wonder if the world was coming to an end.

Despite the suffering they endured, those who lived with the storms managed to cope—hating them, but withstanding them. Many saw themselves as pioneers, battling to survive in frontier conditions and not expecting life to be an easy road. Others took comfort from the fact that the storms were not constant, that there were many calm days, and that they were where they wanted to be—on the land, among friends and family. As one Kansas woman remarked, "Why do we stay? In part because we hope for the coming of moisture, which would change conditions so that we again would have bountiful harvests. And in great part, because it is home. We have reared our family here and have many precious memories of the past. . . . We have faith in the future, we are here to stay."[49]

In the Calm

Dust storms that shut down all activities were usually fairly brief events. After them the sky would clear, the sun would shine, and normal life would resume. The wind might not die completely, but residents of the plains were used to ordinary winds that ranged from gentle breezes to steady blows.

Most people got used to having some dust in the air, too, even on calm days. But with plenty of work to do, no one sat around and thought about it for too long. Terry Clipper of Dustin, Oklahoma, explained:

> We never sat down. . . . We were up early in the morning and gone till late at night, especially my dad and I. The girls . . . had to get up early and milk and they'd milk at night. On rainy days if we weren't in school especially on a Saturday or Sunday when we couldn't be out in the field working because it was raining, [dad would] send us to the barn to shuck corn.[50]

"Burning Up"

There were few rainy days during the drought of the 1930s. High temperatures added to farmers' troubles and made even calm days unbearably hot. A record temperature was set in Nebraska in 1934, when an official reading of 118 degrees was taken. Other plains locales recorded temperatures above 110 that lasted for weeks at a time. Even the nights were hot, making sleep difficult. Some people slept outside on porches or lawns. Townspeople who had electricity could purchase electric fans that at least provided some circulation, but farm families could only hang wet towels about the house and imagine that they felt cooler.

Heat and drought sapped energy from every living thing. As Ann Marie Low wrote, "The crops which hadn't blown had baked in the ground. There would be no grain to cut and shuck. The garden never came up. There was no corn to cultivate; it had not come up either. The hay meadows were rapidly burning up in the hot sun."[51]

Those farmers who did have crops had to neglect them while they hauled water for their livestock. When streams dried up, springs stopped bubbling, and cattle clustered around waterless water holes, farmers were forced to draw buckets of water from the family well and carry them to the fields. Melt White remembered what was, for him, a tedious chore:

> We had a team and we had water barrels. We hauled stock water and household water both. . . . And lots of mornin's we'd get up and strain our drinkin' water like people strain milk, through a cloth, to strain the debris out of it. But then, of course, a lotta grit went through and settled to the bottom of the bucket, but you

had [to] have drinkin' water. And when you got you a little dipper of water, you drink it. You didn't take a sip and throw it away, because it was a very precious thing to us because we had to haul it.[52]

Lack of water was not the only problem. With a shortage of feed, some farmers resorted to feeding their cattle Russian thistles, also known as tumbleweed. These they made more palatable by sprinkling them with molasses. Some southern farmers gathered prickly pear cactus, burned off the thorns, and fed their animals those. The substitutes did not provide adequate nourishment, however, and the animals became emaciated. Some dropped dead from hunger and heat. Some had to be shot. Others were shipped to market, but as historian Vance Johnson notes, supply quickly overcame demand. "Trainload upon trainload poured into Kansas City. The livestock market was demoralized. The livestock exchange broadcast an appeal to farmers to withhold shipments; packers could not handle the cattle that were being offered for sale. But still the cattle came."[53]

Children in Colorado cover their mouths as they pump water during a dust storm. Lack of water was a very serious problem for most dust bowl farmers.

Cattle and horses were not the only ones to die as a result of the heat. Thousands of humans died of heat-related causes as well. Ann Marie Low noted statistics in 1931: "The heat deaths in the country total 1,231. I mean humans. Lord only knows how many animals have died."[54] In 1935, at least one farmer—only twenty-three years old—fell dead in his fields after working in the one-hundred-plus degree sunshine.

"Sunup to Sundown"

It was a wonder more farmers did not die from their labors. A normal workday was grueling, beginning before dawn and ending after dusk. Cows had to be milked and farm animals fed before breakfast. Fields had to be planted in the spring, tended in the summer, and harvested in the fall.

There was other fieldwork to do, too. For instance, once wheat was cut, it had to be piled, bundled, and later threshed and winnowed—a process that separated grain from chaff. With meager harvests, most small farmers could manage this alone. Able-bodied family members were always willing to pitch in, too. Many schools closed for six weeks during harvest time so children could help gather the crops. Vera Criswell recalled, "I was in the field from sunup to sundown. . . . It was just

A cattle skull sits on parched earth in South Dakota. Many dust bowl cattle died from hunger and heat.

A Kansas farmer removes mud from a watering tank. Even during severe dust storms, farmers had no choice but to carry out their daily chores.

something I'd done all my life and I didn't know any different. Most of my friends and everybody around me did the same things. It was a way of life in those days on the farm. It was just the way that people lived."[55]

In addition to caring for crops and livestock, there were all kinds of maintenance projects. Fences and roads had to be kept in repair. Houses, barns, and outbuildings needed to be weatherized against the coming winter. Chicken runs and poultry cages had to be cleaned, wood hauled and chopped, trips to town for supplies made in the family's rattletrap jalopy.

There was always extra work to be done after a dust storm moved through. Cows had to be currycombed clean before they could be milked. Root cellars where vegetables were stored had to be dug out of drifts. Fences that were buried in dirt had to be raised; others had to be reset because all the dirt around them had been blown away. Cattle that had wandered out of fields had to be rounded up.

Homemakers

Men were not the only hard workers in the family. In addition to cooking and cleaning, raising the children and managing the household, farm women made their own soap and churned their own butter. Because nine out of ten homes were without electric service or indoor plumbing, women drew all the water

Without laborsaving devices, farm women worked hard at chores such as washing clothes. The first step was to soak dirty garments in a huge copper pot of water that had been heated on the stove. Ann Marie Low describes the rest of the process in *Dust Bowl Diary*.

"Most farm women had to scrub their clothes by hand on a wash board, but we had a wooden tub with an agitator inside, which we ran by pulling back and forth a handle on the side of the tub. We cranked a wringer by hand to rid the clothes of the soapy water as they went into the rinse water.

After the clothes were boiled, one of us would agitate them ten or fifteen minutes in the washing machine, then wring them into a tub of warm rinse water. We had filled the machine and that tub with warm water from the reservoir of the cookstove and kettles of water heated on top of the stove.

From the warm rinse we wrung the clothes into a tub of cold rinse filled with pails of water carried directly from the cistern. . . . Then we moved the wringer again to squeeze out the water and let the clothes drop into the clothes basket, which we carried to the clothesline west of the house. . . .

When the washing was done, we emptied the machine and tubs and put them away, saving the soapy water for scrubbing floors. Making soap and carrying water were work—we did not waste soapy water. We did not waste any water, in fact, but used the rinse water on the plants."

they used from a well or cistern and heated it over a wood- or coal-burning stove. They washed clothes on a washboard and hung them on lines to dry. They scrubbed floors on hands and knees, canned their own vegetables, made feather beds and pillows from down plucked from their own poultry, and sewed everything from dresses to curtains to quilts on pedal-operated sewing machines.

Although many farm women had little education past the eighth grade, they had plenty of common sense and a wealth of information learned from their mothers. Medical information was vital: Most women treated their family's ailments with home remedies such as senna tea for constipation, mulligan leaves and whiskey for coughs, and mustard plasters for colds. James Lambert remembered that a mustard plaster "burnt like hell when it was put on your chest, 'cause you wore it all night. The stink was horrible but it would knock a

cold out and of course for most of the sickness there was castor oil."[56]

Doctors were often some distance away, so many women relied on midwives when they gave birth. These women, who had much experience delivering babies, were competent in normal situations, but if complications occurred, many mothers and babies died. Talmage Collins of Jasper, Arkansas, recalled, "The first funeral I can remember was the sister of my uncle's wife. She died in childbirth at home with no doctor and no midwife. . . . They had a funeral, and she was buried in the backyard right outside the bedroom."[57]

School Days

Despite infant mortality, farm families were usually large, with ten or more children. Because school attendance became mandatory in every state by the end of the 1920s, most of these children were sent to school at about the age of six.

Rural schools were usually one-room buildings equipped with simple desks, a wood stove for heat, and an outhouse in the backyard. If districts were very poor, books and paper were scarce, and chalkboards were nothing but boards painted black. With only one teacher per school, students learned the basics of reading, writing, and arithmetic, and little more. Oklahoman Elbert Garretson observed, "The teachers were real good under the conditions. We had all eight grades in one room with one teacher part of the time which

was difficult. One of the teachers was kind of cruel. . . . Some of the boys got a spanking every day and sometimes a hair snatching or a pulling . . . I thought he was a fine old fellow but he still missed the mark."[58]

Even getting through eighth grade was an accomplishment to be proud of if one was needed to help on the farm. "Almost every year I'd miss some school because we just wouldn't be through [harvesting] by the time [classes] took up,"[59] remembered Vera Criswell, who only went as far as the first year of high school. Not only was a child's absence from the workforce a hardship for most parents, but school clothes and shoes were extra expenses as well. Hattye Shields of McIntosh

Dust bowl children like this young boy divided their time between attending school and working in the fields.

County, Oklahoma, recalled, "I remember we had one pair of shoes in the fall and that was to start school with. . . . You had to make that one pair last till the next spring until it got warm enough to go barefoot. . . . Mother would make dresses for us to go to school out of flour sacks. In those days they had those nice printed flour sacks and that's what we wore to school."[60]

Getting a higher education was almost impossible with family responsibilities and no money. Nevertheless, going to college remained a top priority for some families. "Mama's heart is set on good educations for her children," wrote Ann Marie Low. "Dad wants that, too."[61] With hard work and sacrifice on everyone's part, all three of the Low children—like other young people in the region—were able to attend college and thus realize their and their parents' dreams.

"The Same Old Business"

Despite school responsibilities, older children were often required to look after younger ones as well as help with the chores while their mother and father did other farmwork. And older daughters were valuable assistants when it came to cleaning house after a dust storm. On those days, farm women liked to clean their homes thoroughly from top to bottom. Some homes were large and well furnished, but most small farmers could afford only a small wood-framed structure that included a large kitchen, a parlor (living room), and several bedrooms. Furniture was limited to a worn sofa, a large wooden table and chairs in the kitchen, and several double beds. Dishes sat on open shelves, clothes hung on pegs, and an outhouse in the backyard served as a bathroom.

Whether a house was large or small, after storms women swept—and sometimes shov-

eled out—floors and then scrubbed them. They washed and wiped walls. They polished windows. They removed dust from furniture. They wiped shelves, washed dishes, and laundered bedclothes. If a home was large, as was the case with the Low family, the cleanup could take hours and became extremely tedious when it was performed repeatedly. Ann Marie Low wrote, "The same old business of scrubbing floors in all nine rooms, washing all the woodwork and windows, washing the bedding, curtains, and towels, taking all the rugs and sofa pillows out to beat the dust out of them, cleaning closets and cupboards, dusting all the books and furniture, washing the mirrors and every dish and cooking utensil."[62]

Life in Town

In towns, life was somewhat easier than on a farm. Electricity made labor-saving devices like vacuum cleaners, refrigerators, and washing machines available. People were not as isolated—friends, neighbors, and even doctors were nearby to help in time of emergency.

Most small towns were communities clustered around a main street lined with a few businesses, including a post office, a bank, a café, and a drug store with a soda fountain. Most towns could boast a church or two, a school, and sometimes a railroad station and a theater. There were stores where women could buy brooms and mops when theirs wore out from all the cleaning. There were car repair shops where dirt-choked automobile engines could be cleaned. There also were enterprising entrepreneurs, such as one Dodge City man who earned a living cleaning dust out of attics for overworked homemakers.

Town homes were often built better than farmhouses, too, and some had cellars in

Party Line

Few rural families had electricity, but most had a telephone, which eased their isolation from the outside world. Party lines—where several families shared the same circuit and could thus listen in on each other's conversations—were common then, as Ann Marie Low remembers in her book, *Dust Bowl Diary*.

"We had wall telephones with a crank at the side to ring them. All rings were heard by everyone on the party line. Everyone knew just who was being called because each ring was different. Ours, I recall, was a long ring followed by a short ring. The Scotts were called by three short rings and the Brewer family by two longs and two shorts. It did not matter who was called; all the neighbors listened in. This was called 'rubbernecking' and was the main amusement and diversion of the rural housewife.

Central [the operator], a vital part of the community, always knew where everybody was and what was going on. In case of disaster or emergency, just as 'Johnson's little boy is missing' or 'Hannan's barn is on fire,' Central used the general ring, a series of long rings, to summon the people on all the party lines to drop what they were doing and go to help."

which people took shelter during the worst storms. "I had one of the nicest storm cellars you ever walked into," remembered Robert Dinwiddie, who left Oklahoma during the dust bowl. "It was a large one. You could put twenty people in it. It was concrete all up and down. Inside the cellar we had shelves built in where you could set food. We had a full size bed in there, too."[63]

Simple Pleasures

Even if a town was no more than a main street and a general store, it attracted farm families who brought eggs and butter to market regularly. For farm families, "going to town" was a highlight of their week. If nothing more, it was a time to enjoy the comings and goings of other people, look in store windows, and maybe buy a soda at the soda fountain. Oklahoman James Lackey remembered, "Every Saturday night, everybody went to town. You could see them setting up on the street. Guys up there whittling and smoking cigars. Saturday night was the main event. You worked all the time, but Saturday night was your night."[64]

Other than a trip to town, there was little entertainment for farm families to enjoy. In the evenings, many relied on books and the local newspaper to pass the time, although bedtimes came early after a long day of work. Some families enjoyed music. Talmage Collins of Arkansas recalled, "Sometimes they'd sing, pick guitar, play banjo, pop popcorn or play cards. . . . They played a game they called pitch. You played it with a deck of cards. Or they played dominos or checkers."[65]

Community activities were also popular and usually centered around church. Whether Baptist, Methodist, or some other denomination, almost everyone attended church on Sunday and often throughout the week. "I started singing in the church choir when I was twelve," remembered Juanita Price. "The choir rehearsals were on Friday nights so we'd work hard all day, come home and clean up, and then we'd go to rehearsals. I just enjoyed that."[66]

Because everyone was poor, church social events were simple and inexpensive. Revivals, during which an evangelist would visit the community and lead a series of inspirational services, were a good chance to see neighbors and friends. Eating together was also a good way to socialize. Price recalled, "Church suppers was a deal where everybody would come to the church and bring food and then they'd sell the food. They'd call it pie suppers if they sold pie. And they sold cakes, cookies, donuts or whatever. I used to enjoy that so much to get away from the monotony of our poor existence."[67]

Those who lived in town had other entertainment options, too. Libraries provided pleasure for those who loved to read. Ethel Bellezzuoli of Duncan, Oklahoma, remembered, "I'd walk to the library every day and get two books. I'd read them and then I would go back the next day."[68] Men joined service organizations such as the Rotary Club and the Kiwanis Club, while women formed bridge clubs and attended plays put on by local drama clubs. Some communities had a baseball team that competed with neighboring towns. Sometimes the ball was hard to see for the dust, but the games went on except during the worst storms.

One unique pastime for entire families was gathering arrowheads left by Native American tribes that had once inhabited the Great Plains. The artifacts were uncovered after strong storms blew away topsoil, and interested families passed sunny Sunday afternoons by packing a picnic lunch and going out to look for them. William Ellmore Baker, who lived in Boise City, Oklahoma, was more serious in his searching. As the dust blew, he was able to locate hundreds of sites and collect

"Hog Heaven"

On the Great Plains, the phrase "hog heaven" described a state of bliss that was higher than mere happiness. With few good things in life, special foods could provoke such great excitement, as Loye Holmes describes in Oral History Interviews sponsored by California State University, Bakersfield, and found on the university library's website at www.lib.csub.edu:

"We took our eggs to town. We would pack our eggs in a tub in cotton seed to keep them from breaking because we went to town in wagons. We also took our cream to town. . . . We used the money from the cream and eggs to buy staples. The main things we bought were salt, sugar, baking powder and coffee.

My mother made sure she had her coffee—Peaberry brand. You couldn't fool her. You could try every way to give her some other coffee but she always knew if it was Peaberry or not. . . .

If we were able to get a loaf of light bread that was like dessert to us. My mother did have a friend that she'd got acquainted with when we had our shoe shop. They had a grocery store and restaurant. She would sometimes save the bread heels for my mother in a flour sack. My mother would bring them home on Saturday night as a treat for us kids. She'd say, 'Let's let them last two or three days. Don't eat too many of them.' She'd make bread puddings and we thought we were in hog heaven."

Church parishioners in New Mexico sing during a Sunday service. Churches throughout the dust bowl organized activities to provide communities with entertainment.

thousands of arrowheads and other artifacts within a fifty-mile radius of his home in the Oklahoma panhandle, becoming one of the top archaeologists of his day.

The Younger Generation

Children's pastimes was as simple as those enjoyed by their elders. Little girls played dolls and house. Boys were outside in all but the worst storms, shooting marbles, climbing trees, and the like. "We . . . made kites," said Herman Lawson:

We tied two light-weight sticks together to form a cross. Then we attached a string around the end of the cross sticks in the shape of a diamond. A piece of newspaper was cut a little larger than the diamond, folded over and pasted with paste made from Mom's flour bin. Attach a tail of old rags and it was ready to fly. We usually didn't have to wait long for the wind to blow.[69]

Young people of dating age were fortunate if a movie theater was located in a nearby town. Schools also hosted parties where students could play games or dance, although many parents frowned on dancing for religious reasons.

There were fewer marriages in the 1930s than in any other decade in U.S. history, but young men and women still fell in love and got married. Many couples could trace their attraction for each other back to their grammar school days. "I met [my husband] the first year I started school," recalled Loye Holmes of Wayside, Oklahoma. "I was six . . . and my husband was four years older than me. . . . My sister liked his older brother. My sister two years older than me liked his brother who was two years older than him. We wound up marrying those boys."[70]

Despite the limited fun they had, the younger generation did not consider themselves cursed by fate or the weather. Wind, dust, and poverty were the only things they knew. The worst storms were scary and uncomfortable, but they also provided excitement and drew people closer together. Hattye Shields observed, "I remember it being a fun time. When you're young a farm is fun because you've got animals and we had a lot of brothers and sisters and mine were all older except for one. So it was a fun time living on a farm. It was hard that we didn't have anything. We really had nothing. . . . That was just a way of life."[71]

That philosophical attitude was one of the reasons that so many people remained in the region. After all, there were some advantages of living on a farm during the Great Depression. Those who had chickens and cows knew that they always had food. If they could not sell their wheat or corn, at least they could grind it up and bake it into bread.

Then, too, most were convinced that a season of good rain would set things right again. The words "if it rains" came to symbolize the stubborn optimism of those who remained on the land in the face of all kinds of hardships. Dean Banker remembered, "Every day they'd say, 'Well, it's going to rain today. Surely it will rain today. Or maybe tomorrow.' There was always this eternal optimism. And I don't know where that came from unless it was the pioneer spirit. . . . It was a tremendous test of stick-to-itivness. We didn't know you weren't not supposed to stay."[72]

CHAPTER
4 If It Rains

Years of drought, heat, and dust took their toll on dust bowl residents, but these were not the only trials people had to face during the 1930s. Winters were bitterly cold. Fire, insects, and other pests often swept the region. Loved ones died of illness or injury. Nevertheless, mutual support, humor, and the optimistic belief that the rains would come kept people going. Imogene Glover said, "My daddy was an optimist. I think he just kept thinking, 'Next year will be better and we'll have a good crop and we'll raise some more cattle and we'll get rich.' We never did, but he thought we would."[73]

Blizzards and Snusters

There were plenty of challenges in addition to dust storms to test the optimism of plains residents during the 1930s. At times, it seemed as if all the forces of nature were against them.

Even in the midst of drought, afternoon thunderstorms could produce hail that beat down entire fields of wheat and oats in just a few minutes. In 1935 in Cimarron County, Oklahoma, one storm dropped cue ball–size hail that broke windows and killed livestock. Glenn McMurry, who lived in Kansas, described his own frightening experience:

We had been watching a storm coming in from the west, but had no idea it was coming so fast. As I was coming back from the [grain] elevator, about a mile from home, a rolling cloud closed up on me. I had all I could do to guide the truck on the road. By the time I got to the driveway, the wind was whipping the trees around violently. It was raining hard and in the rain were hailstones as big as large marbles. The sound of the hail on the top of my truck was like rocks on a tin roof.[74]

Sparked by lightning, prairie fires could sweep across fields and burn crops and farm buildings to the ground in a moment's time. When word of a fire went around, everyone in the vicinity turned out to try to put out the flames with sand and wet gunnysacks. One inexperienced firefighter used other means, as Ann Marie Low recalled: "He took his trousers off to beat out the fire. That ended his trousers; the fire roared on like Hell's delight."[75]

Unsettled weather in the spring and fall was prone to spawn tornadoes that could whirl over farms, leaving ruin in their wake. Glenn McMurry remembered, "We found the large barn demolished, the old garage down and practically every old cedar tree in our front yard uprooted! Destruction was everywhere, but luckily there was no major damage to the house itself."[76]

Winter weather could be just as severe. Bone-chilling winds and snowstorms swept the plains. Ann Marie Low wrote, "Last weekend a bad blizzard struck and it snowed so much all week we couldn't get to school at

Dust storms were not the only force of nature to plague dust bowl residents.
Lightning storms and tornadoes also caused significant damage to property and crops.

all. Dad and [my brother] Bud and I had a real struggle getting the cattle in from the hills in that blinding snow."[77] Sometimes the winds accompanying such blizzards whipped dirt high in the air, creating what became known as a "snuster"—a mixture of snow and dust. One such storm on April 7, 1938, killed hundreds of livestock and left travelers stranded across five states.

Plagues and Pests

In addition to weather, farmers regularly combated invasions of insects. Potato bugs were common pests that could ruin a flourishing potato crop. Low remembered,

> Monday Dad was out in the potato field knocking potato bugs off the plants into a pail. He was going to kill them by pouring kerosene over them. When a sudden hailstorm came up, he set the pail down in the barnyard so he could help with the terrified horses. A horse kicked the bucket over. Several thousand of Dad's little jewels went back to the potato field.[78]

Potato bugs were only one kind of insect that farmers combated. Boll weevils destroyed cotton crops. Armyworms ate grain. Grasshoppers were more destructive than either. The dry heat caused billions of grasshoppers to hatch, and they swept over farms, filled the sky, darkened the sun, and chewed everything from corn in the field to clothes on the line. Journalist Ernie Pyle noted after a trip through South Dakota,

> A cornfield after grasshoppers get through with it looks like a freshly plowed field, just after the soil is turned and is all black and rich-looking, with no vegetation

at all. They not only strip the blades; they eat the stalk, and burrow down into the ground and nibble away the roots. They leave nothing on the surface whatever. They do the same with grain and grass and vegetables.[79]

One farmer estimated that grasshoppers numbered almost twenty-four thousand per acre on his place. In some areas, they lay inches deep on city streets and were so thick that their bodies clogged car radiators and caused train wheels to slip on railroad tracks. Some people tried to kill them with poison, while others simply waited until they ate their fill and moved on. Low wrote, "Uncle George says he bugs the potatoes twice a day but has to kick the grasshoppers out of the way first. He says the Bakers have lost 100 acres of corn to the grasshoppers and have quit cultivating because they are tired of giving the hoppers a ride around the field."[80]

Jackrabbits were almost as thick as grasshoppers. Some people believed that the hot weather caused the rodents to multiply; others claimed they moved into the area looking for food. Whatever the reason, hundreds of thousands appeared on the plains, eating anything that grew. Lloyd Chance, who farmed near Woods, Kansas, said, "I've seen [rabbits] start at the edge of a wheat field and soon work their way into it, stripping it as they went."[81]

Residents knew how to combat this kind of plague. Rabbit hunts were organized, and on many Sunday afternoons, hundreds of people turned out to drive the animals into quickly constructed corrals where they were beaten to death with clubs. (Guns were not used because the danger of accidentally shooting one's neighbor was too great.) The drives were a brutal, yet effective way of reducing the rabbit population; sometimes as

Removing a Grasshopper

Few dust bowl residents recorded their feelings about having grasshoppers land on their skin or get caught up in their clothes. In a rare account included in "The Autobiography of an Unimportant Important Man," found on the Resolution Productions website, Glenn D. McMurry describes what happened while he and his cousin Gene were driving a stripped-down truck on the family farm.

"Gene was touchy and nervous about getting grasshoppers in his clothes. When one got into his pants as we were driving along, he took immediate action. You would have thought a four-foot rattlesnake was in his pants the way he acted.

[This time,] without any warning to me to stop or even slow the truck, Gene stood straight up on his side of the gas tank seat, let out a wild bellow, and stepped onto the running board of the truck. Then making desperate motions with his arms, he tried to extract the insect from his pants. It didn't matter to him whether it was a little grasshopper or a big one. It had to be removed promptly.

In the process, Gene lost his balance and fell from the running-board directly onto the ground below! Although the speed of my truck was less than ten miles per hour by this time, it was still fast enough to throw him down on the ground flat on his face directly in line with the on-coming rear truck wheel.

The wheel passed right over his body. I was petrified!

After stopping the truck as quickly as I could, I rushed back to help him up. I was very happy to find that he really didn't need any help. He was already up on his feet, grinning, brushing the dust and sand from his hair and clothes as though it was all a normal procedure for removing a grasshopper from pants!"

many as two thousand rabbits were killed at a time. After the kill, the animals provided meat for many poor families and could be sold for fur and pet food in order to bring in a little extra cash.

Under the Weather

Dust bowl families faced more than bad weather and insect invasions. All had to deal with normal tribulations of life such as childhood diseases—measles, mumps, chickenpox, diphtheria, and whooping cough—which struck regularly. Women died in childbirth. Men died from untreated injuries. Conditions such as pneumonia, diabetes, and heart disease were common, too, and because they were ineffectively treated with home remedies, some people lived in a state of chronic ill health and died young. The loss of a loved one was just one more burden that already over-burdened families had to bear.

Some illnesses were a direct result of exposure to dust. Fine silicon particles—similar to those that caused black lung disease in coal miners—were present in the dirt, and when they were inhaled they cut and irritated the mucous membranes of the respiratory system. "Dust pneumonia," a condition in which dust irritated the lungs and bronchial tubes and led to infection and sometimes death, was extremely common during this time. J.R. Davison of Texas remembered, "I was pretty small when I got the dust pneumonia. I don't remember exactly getting sick, but I do remember part of my stay in the hospital. They took me to Amarillo, that was the closest good hospital, and I guess I was sicker than I ever realized, because I got . . . delirious."[82]

In the spring of 1935, the U.S. Public Health Service noted a 50 to 100 percent increase in pneumonia over the same months in 1934. Other respiratory conditions such as sinusitis, laryngitis, and bronchitis were also more common. Many people suffered from strep throat and eye infections, and, perhaps as a result of swallowing so much dirt, many people developed appendicitis as well. Charles Newsome of Fort Gibson, Oklahoma, recalled, "My dad had an acute attack of appendicitis . . . and had to be rushed to the hospital and I guess his appendix had ruptured and he had peritonitis [inflammation of the

A swarm of grasshoppers moves across a dry plain. These pests and others devoured acres of dust bowl crops.

abdominal lining]. He was at the hospital for a long time. I don't know how much it cost but it set us way back."[83]

Hospitals provided oxygen to help those who had respiratory difficulties, but many who were not strong died. The death rate in forty-five dust-stricken western counties in Kansas was 99 deaths per 100,000 compared to an average of 70 per 100,000 across the state. The infant death rate was more than 80 per 100,000 compared to a state average of just over 62.

Even those who did not develop medical conditions felt the physical effects of inhaling so much dust. People coughed and spat up mud. One farmer, Lawrence Svobida, said, "The dust I had labored in all day began to show its effects on my system. My head ached, my stomach was upset, and my lungs were oppressed and felt as if they must contain a ton of fine dirt."[84]

Leaning on Each Other

People had plenty of problems in the dust bowl, but those problems did not appear so overwhelming when one had family and friends to turn to in the worst difficulties. Parents, sisters, brothers, uncles, aunts, and

A mother gives her young boy a dose of cod liver oil. Some dust bowl residents developed serious medical conditions as a result of the dust storms.

cousins often lived within a few miles of each other, so there was always someone to talk to or ask for help. When fields needed to be listed (plowed with equipment that piled dirt on both sides of the furrow) in order to reduce erosion, farmers shared equipment. When illness or injury struck, relatives took over farm chores, brought in food, and took care of small children. Newlywed Juanita Price remembered helping out after her parents separated and her mother left the family in 1932. "My little brothers and sisters was home and I'd be back over to their house about every two or three days. . . . My sister-in-law and I would go over there, cook a big meal for them, comb their heads, bathe them and help clean up the house."[85]

Neighbors and friends were also a source of support and comfort in times of crisis. "Everybody helped," remembered Vera Criswell, "If I had something that somebody else could use I gave it to them. If it hadn't been for people helping one another I don't know what we would have done."[86]

Last Man's Club

The faith and optimism of many dust bowl residents were apparent in decisions they made to remain and go on with their lives despite the hard times. Many got married and began building their futures together. Some expanded their businesses. Chorla Basset, a grandmother who lost her husband in 1934, took a job as a nurse for an elderly woman with a broken hip near Boise City, Oklahoma. When that job ended, Basset went on to become an Avon perfume sales agent and then bought and ran a variety store in the area.

Many dust bowl residents were indignant when outsiders drew national attention to the devastation of the dust bowl.

Can't Kill Me

One of Woody Guthrie's most popular songs was "Dust Can't Kill Me," written in 1938. The complete lyrics, which express the pain and defiant pride of those who were fighting for their lives in the dust bowl, can be found at the Geocities website (www.geocities.com).

That old dust storm killed my baby,
Can't kill me, Lord, can't kill me.
That old dust storm got my family,
Can't get me, Lord, can't get me.

That old landlord got my homestead,
Can't get me, Lord, can't get me.
That old dry spell killed my crops, boys,
Can't kill me, no, it can't kill me. . . .

That old pawn shop got my furniture,
Can't get me, Lord, can't get me.
That old highway got my relatives,
Can't get me, Lord, can't get me.

That old dust might kill my wheat, boys,
Can't kill me, Lord, can't kill me.
I have weathered many a dust storm,
Can't kill me, Lord, can't kill me.

That old dust storm will have blowed
my barn down,
But it can't blow me down, it can't blow
me.
That old wind might blow this world
down,
Can't blow me down, can't kill me.

We Stayed

Many people remained in the dust bowl through the hard times because they had no other option. In the PBS special "Surviving the Dust Bowl," accessed on the PBS website (www.pbs.org), Melt White describes the situation he and his family faced during that time.

"I've seen desperate looks on Dad's face. He had lots of stamina. He didn't seem to—he didn't show discouragement. He didn't show disappointment. He always . . . he lived with hopes. 'Next year. Next year. I failed this time, but next year'll be better.' And I never did see him have the look of givin' up or quitting. . . . He always stayed in there and seemed that he was gonna make it some way

or another. If anybody made it, he'd be one of 'em, he thought.

The reason why we stayed, the reason my dad stayed, we didn't have a wherewith to do with. We had no reserve, had no money. We had no automobile. We had teams, but where could we go? Ah, 'cause at that time a hundred miles in a team wagon was a good long ways. It was like I said a while ago. It took eight days to come from Los Alamos to Colorado to Dalhart with a team and wagon. So where would we go? We had nowhere to go or nothin' to go with. So—and he had this little job with the WPA and he went to gettin' his little $16-a-month pension. So he figured it was best to stay with what he had, because he didn't know where to go to get anything any better."

That attention included the government film *The Plow That Broke the Plains*, whose music evoked a strong emotional response, and sensational magazine articles such as Walter Davenport's "Land Where Our Children Die," which focused on the worst of conditions and made them seem universal. Davenport described the dust bowl as a place of "famine, violent death, private and public futility, insanity, and lost generations."[87]

In the opinion of the dust bowlers, journalists and politicians were out of line when they reported widespread destitution and despair. As one writer for the Springfield, Colorado, *Democrat-Herald* observed,

Last week the big press associations broke with a big yarn [story] about the dust pneumonia with which many of our citizens have been afflicted and by the time the stories reached New York and

Los Angeles it appears that most of us were dead or dying. . . . To the folks from out of the county we can truthfully say that it has been plenty bad here but not as terrible as the eastern and far western headline writers would have you believe.[88]

Some people, like John McCarty, editor of the *Dalhart Texan*, even decided to take a public stand against the negative press. In 1935, when rumors were rampant that the government was contemplating the widespread forced resettlement of farmers so that the land could be replanted and preserved, McCarty decided he would not desert the region. In his newspaper, he published a pledge that he would stay even if he were the last man left. Calling the plains "the best damned country God's sun ever shown upon,"[89] he dared others to join him in his stand. Approximately one hundred farmers, bankers, business owners, schoolteachers, cowboys, and mechanics took the challenge to stay in their dusty homeland. As they filed into McCarty's office and shook his hand, "The Last Man's Club" was formed. It held no meetings, charged no dues, and adopted only one resolution: "In the absence of an act of God, serious family injury, or some other emergency, I pledge to stay here as the last man and to do everything I can to help other last men remain in this country. We promise to stay here 'til hell freezes over and skate out on the ice."[90] By its existence alone, the club inspired many people to stay and fight dust and drought until better conditions returned.

Dust Humor

While some people expressed their optimism through defiance, others turned to humor. Jokes and tall tales that made light of the wind and the dirt crisscrossed the plains. Dust bowl residents reportedly tested the wind's velocity by tying a chain to a tree. If the chain blew out straight, the day was calm. If it cracked like a whip, a heavy breeze was blowing. If it snapped to pieces and the tree came out by the roots, a blizzard or twister was raging.

The jokes were corny, but produced much laughter. Farmers claimed they gathered up the postholes that were left standing above the ground after a heavy duster so they would not have to dig them again. One claimed he watched birds fly backwards to keep the sand out of their eyes. Another said he shot ground squirrels as they burrowed up through the air. Photojournalist Margaret Bourke-White told of a pilot who had to parachute out of his plane in a dust storm. He had taken six hours to shovel his way to the ground.

One of the most oft-told jokes was the account of a man who, in the midst of the drought, was hit in the face with a drop of rain and fainted. Two buckets of sand, thrown in his face, revived him. Another popular story involved a motorist who saw a ten-gallon hat lying alongside the road. Picking it up, he found a man's head underneath. The motorist asked if he could help in some way, perhaps by giving the man a ride into town. The man answered, "Thanks, but I'll make it on my own. I'm on a horse."[91]

Some of the humor was off-the-cuff, as when a farmer was asked what he was doing as he sat on his front porch in Nebraska in the middle of a dust storm. "I'm counting the Kansas farms as they go by,"[92] he answered. Another farmer said to a friend, "I hope it'll rain before the kids grow up. They ain't never seen none."[93]

Voice of the Dust Bowl

Singer Woodrow Wilson "Woody" Guthrie captured some of the melancholy humor of the dust bowl in songs that he wrote about the people and the problems of the Great Plains. For instance, in his song "Dust Pneumonia Blues," he sang,

> Now there ought to be some yodelin' in this song;
>
> Yeah, there ought to be some yodelin' in this song;
>
> But I can't yodel for the rattlin' in my lung.[94]

Born in Okemah, Oklahoma, Guthrie took to the road at the age of sixteen and experienced hardship, poverty, dust storms, and drought. He identified with the victims of the Great Depression and wrote many songs that put their feelings into words. Guthrie's dust bowl ballads include "Dust Can't Kill Me," "Blowin' Down the Road," and "Dusty Old Dust (So Long, It's Been Good to Know You)," which described the Black Sunday dust storm. Whether whimsical or serious, most of Guthrie's songs paid tribute to the toughness of working people who refused to give in to the hard times. "They are 'Oakie' songs," Guthrie explained. "'Migratious' songs, about my folks and my relatives, about a jillion of 'em, that got hit by the drouth [drought], the dust, the wind, the banker, and the landlord, and the police all at the same time."[95]

Guthrie sang about not only those who stuck it out in the dust bowl, but those who left

Woody Guthrie wrote a number of songs about the people and problems of the dust bowl.

the area, either because they had to or because they believed a better life awaited them elsewhere. For those who moved, travel was difficult. Many had no money to pay for food, lodging, and car repairs along the way. They had to scrimp and stop often to find work to pay for such essentials. Then, at the end of the journey, most discovered that money did not come easily, even in California, the golden state where orange juice, sunshine, and jobs were reportedly plentiful. As Earl Butler observed, "In most cases, most of them would have probably been better off if they'd stayed put. It was a case of GO WEST. The future was there, the work plentiful and the wages good. [But] it wasn't that way when you got there. . . . Most of the people were farm people and didn't really know the ways of the world."[96]

Dusted Out

Dust bowl families were loyal to the plains, but years of bad crops, economic depression, insects, heat, and wind gave some of them little choice but to look for work elsewhere. Even a year of rain and a good harvest could not make up for the monetary loss that many had taken.

Others realized that their dreams were forever beyond reach. Young people who had once planned to go to college saw savings vanish and the opportunity to study disappear while they worked the unprofitable land. Middle-aged couples relinquished plans for a more comfortable home and an inheritance for their children. Old people gave up their homes, turned to public relief (welfare), or resigned themselves to being a burden on their children. Lawrence Svobida, a Kansas wheat farmer, expressed their despair: "My dreams and ambitions had been flouted by nature, and my shattered ideals seemed gone forever."[97]

Some people had borrowed money to buy their land and lost it when they could not pay their mortgage and the bank foreclosed. Some people developed health problems as a result of the dust and could no longer work as hard as they once had. "With my financial resources at last exhausted and my health seriously, if not permanently impaired, I am at last ready to admit defeat and leave the Dust Bowl forever," concluded Svobida, who gave up farming in 1939. "With youth and ambition ground into the very dust itself, I can only drift with the tide."[98]

Grim, Hungry, and Broke

No one knows exactly how many people left the land in the "dirty thirties," but experts believe the total reached 3.5 million people by 1940, with the majority moving after 1935. Oklahoma lost over 18 percent of its 1930 population. Morton County in southwestern Kansas lost 47 percent of its population, and nearby counties experienced similar losses.

Many of those who left were self-sustaining families—that is, those who had had jobs and been well established in the region. Many more, from poor, small family farms, were grim, hungry, and desperate. The men were at their wit's end, needing to provide for their families and humiliated because they could not. Many women were pregnant and wondering how they could support another child. The children were thin, dressed in ragged flour sacks, in poor health. As Talmage Collins wrote, "You got nothing here so you got nothing to lose. That's the way you feel about it. You just take off hoping for the best."[99]

Thousands of the disillusioned moved to a nearby town or county, desiring a fresh start without giving up ties to their region and their state. Some in Kansas, Texas, Oklahoma, and New Mexico took advantage of oil and gas developments in the region, finding work in that industry. Some found jobs in towns like Sunray, Texas, which serviced drilling operations. "We did have an oil based economy which gave some cash flow into an otherwise destitute area. The oil was discovered in '23 and was going pretty good. Even though they were working for let's say $5 a day, that was good wages in the oil patch,"[100] remembered Dean Banker of Russell, Kansas.

Some who left were single men who abandoned family and possessions and hopped on a freight train, traveling from town to town looking for work. Known as hoboes, these individuals slept wherever they could—on back porches, under bridges, or under the stars— and relied on the generosity of others for food and an odd job that could yield a dollar or two. If worse came to worst, they resorted to stealing, as James Lackey remembered: "In Amarillo, we got so hungry that we'd go around and follow the milkman. He'd set a carton of milk on a house step and we'd go get it before daylight to drink it."[101]

Farmworkers walk along the highway toward Los Angeles. Many families left the Great Plains in search of better living conditions elsewhere.

Good-bye Dust Bowl

Although many of the "dusted out" stayed in the region, a large proportion went west,

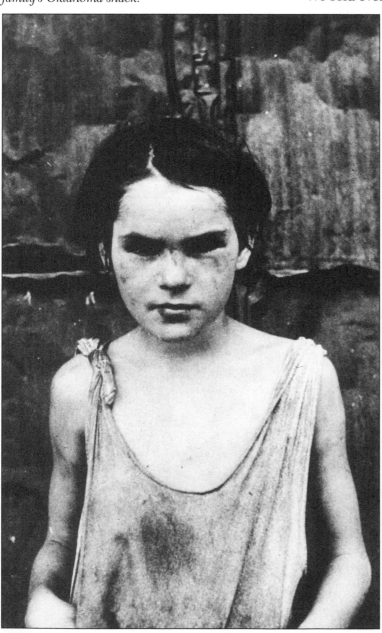

A young girl dressed in rags stands outside of her family's Oklahoma shack.

where work and better times were supposed to be guaranteed. Almost half a million migrated to the Pacific Northwest. Two out of every five went to California, the Golden State, which was known for its agriculture and its job opportunities. Viola Mitchell recalled, "We sold everything we had and got into this Model T Ford truck that my brother had and sixteen of us started out here. There was my mother and dad, their seven children, the man that lived with my parents, and my husband and I and our four babies all in the truck."[102]

Preparations for the moves varied from family to family. One Oklahoma woman quickly roped her few possessions in the back of a truck and with her three children headed off into the unknown. For her, like thousands of others, leaving was a quick decision, with no real destination in mind. Donald Worster described their situation when he wrote:

The people did not stop to shut the door—they just walked out, leaving behind them the wreckage of their labors; an ugly little shack with broken windows covered by cardboard, a sagging ridgepole, a barren, dusty yard, the windmill creaking in the wind. Ten thousand abandoned houses on the high plains; 9 million acres of farmland turned back to nature.[103]

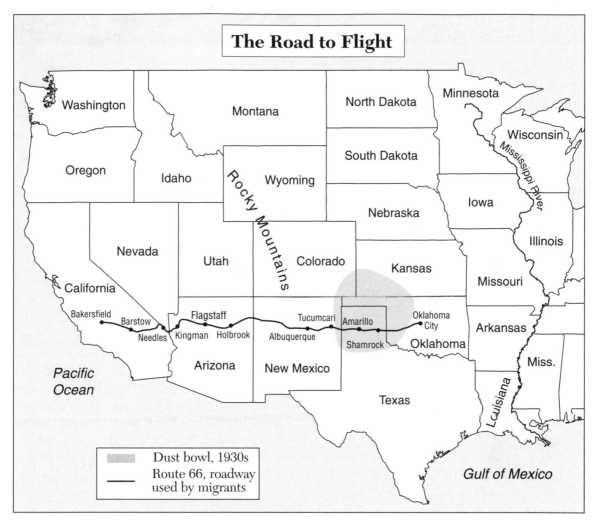

The Road to Flight

Dust bowl, 1930s

Route 66, roadway used by migrants

Other families made more careful plans, such as writing to friends or relatives already in California and selling furniture and livestock they could not carry with them. "I sold my sewing machine, cookstove and bedsteads, and things of that size before we came out," said Juanita Price. "In fact that's how we scraped up enough money to come out here."[104]

Bus, Wagon, or Jalopy

Migrants went west any way that they could. Some, particularly young men who were set-ting out on their own, went by Greyhound bus. Some pushed handcarts or traveled by horse-drawn wagon. "Kids would walk," remembered Talmage Collins. "With the furniture in the wagon you didn't have room for a bunch of kids."[105]

Most, however, traveled by car or truck, although well-worn jalopies were usually in no condition to make such a long trip. Flat tires and overheated engines were common. The weight of a houseful of furniture added to the strain. Somehow families managed to load featherbeds and mattresses, washtubs, pots and pans, children, even small animals

Every migrant family had its own story to tell, but most included a trip westward on Route 66. Such was the case of Paul Westmoreland, whose experiences are included in T.H. Watkins's, *The Hungry Years: A Narrative History of the Great Depression in America.*

"Tens of thousands moved from county to county, state to state, lost in a maze of searching. Paul Westmoreland, who in later life ended up as 'Okie Paul,' a popular disk jockey in Sacramento, California, remembered that his family had been 'starved out' of Oklahoma even before the drought years and had kept on wandering all through the first half of the decade. To Shamrock, Texas, first, to pick cotton; then to Gallup, New Mexico; then from there to Coolidge, Arizona, living off jackrabbits—'Hoover Hogs,' they called them—black-eyed peas, and some pork for side meat. In their old Model-T truck, 'We made twenty-five miles an hour,' he remembered, 'maybe a hundred miles a day going down Route 66, and every other road too, looking for work. We went back to Oklahoma—every good Okie left more than once—and tried again and failed again. Did that more than once until finally we left for good, right down 66, splitting it wide open for six or seven days to Arizona. The wind was blowing, it was dry, the cotton wouldn't come up, everything went wrong.'"

such as dogs and goats. Richard Caudle, who left Oklahoma in 1935, writes,

How could four adults, three kids, a dog named Jiggs, and all our belongings fit into a Model A coupe [sedan]? Daddy, Charles, and Granddaddy soon got it figured out and fixed up. They cut the back out of the car, built a platform with sideboards on it, then bent green sapling trees over the top and covered it with the canvas sacks that would be used for picking cotton. The Model A coupe became a "covered wagon." As much as possible was attached in some way to the outside of the "wagon." The dishes were packed in a five gallon lard can, strapped to the side and nailed down.[106]

Herman Lawson's father had a job waiting in Oregon when the family left Oklahoma in 1937. Lawson, who was thirteen at the time, recalled, "My Dad bought an old house trailer, probably sixteen to eighteen feet long, and ripped out the insides. . . . He placed two double beds at the back end, one over the other. Our gas stove and refrigerator went in the front. . . . My Mom cooked all of our chickens and canned them in half-gallon jars. These, along with some canned vegetables, provided our meals on our trip to our new home."[107]

Route 66

For most migrants, the trip west was made on U.S. Route 66, "the road of flight," as John Steinbeck described it in *The Grapes of Wrath.* An interstate artery that ran from Chicago to Los Angeles, the route was just a two-lane highway made up of bits and pieces of preexisting roads, some concrete, some asphalt, some gravel. It wound through cornfields, deserts, and mountains, cutting across Missouri, Kansas, Oklahoma, Texas, New Mexico, and Arizona.

To those who were used to the flat lands of the plains, the scenery along the route was breathtaking. "I can remember when I first saw the Rocky Mountains. That was really magnificent to see those great big mountains,"[108] said Oscar Kludt, whose family traveled through Wyoming and Nevada to get to California. Joyce Seabolt remembered that her mother was extremely frightened of high elevations:

When we hit New Mexico where we encountered mountains with windy roads, high bridges, steep cliffs, and so forth, my mother refused to go down some of those mountains in the car. She would get out and carry my brother Abe, who was less than a year old, down the steepest hills and let the rest of us go down in the car. . . . My father, who was a very patient man, finally said, "Beulah, we're never going to get to California if you don't stay in the car." . . . She finally consented to stay in the car and not walk down every mountain.[109]

In some places Route 66 ran through the middle of town. In some places filling stations, small restaurants, motels, and cabins for

Migrant families like this one usually carried all of their belongings in a single truck.

rent dotted its shoulders. In other locales, the highway cut across miles and miles of dry, desolate landscape. Ralph Richardson, who owned a gas station in one such region in New Mexico, hung a sign on a cactus that grew along the road. "Carry water or this is what you'll look like,"[110] the sign warned.

Beginning about 1935, a steady stream of migrants made their way westward across the nation. Many joined together in small convoys, supporting each other, especially when breakdowns occurred. "There was a wagon train of us traveling to California. . . . We were always having car trouble," remembered Robert Dinwiddie. "They didn't build good cars in them days. They hadn't learned enough about building cars."[111]

At speeds averaging only thirty-five to forty-five miles an hour, the long trip sometimes took two weeks. If a serious breakdown or an illness occurred, it might take longer. Drivers grimly gripped the steering wheels of their overloaded vehicles and kept an eye out for cheap gasoline. People got sick along the

A migrant family prays before a meal at the side of a highway. Few migrants could afford to stay in motels during their journey.

way. Some pregnant women went into labor and had their babies. "Frightened, those people were frightened, and they came through here thinking they were headed for the Promised Land where they'd say, 'Everything's going to be all right.' I warned them about those ideas, but they went on,"[112] Ralph Richardson, the gas station owner, remembered.

At night, some families with a little extra cash were able to afford a night in a motel. Some spent a dollar to stay in a tourist cabin, which was a small room with beds and a cook stove inside. Others simply camped by the side of the road. Dinner was cooked over an open fire. Washing was done in a stream or ditch if one was nearby. Blankets often served as beds. "We had a brand new tent," recalled Robert Dinwiddie. "One of the other fellows had a tent too. We stretched up them tents and we all lived together in them."[113]

Across the Border

Despite the difficulties, most of the migrants eventually made their way across the country and arrived at the border crossing between Arizona and California. This proved to be a serious obstacle. Many Californians were prejudiced against anyone of a different race, religion, or background, and they were appalled at the number of migrants coming into the state, looking for jobs, and needing welfare. They did not want poor "Okies"—a derogatory term for Oklahomans, but applied to anyone from the dust bowl—dragging down the economy. They did not want Okie children with Midwest accents, patched clothes, and runny noses playing with their children at school. They did not want big Okie families with their jalopies living right next door or down the street.

Well aware of this mind-set, border guards did their best to turn newcomers back. Alvin Laird, who entered California in 1935, stated, "I know this to be the truth—if you didn't have a job or a car they'd turn you back—wouldn't let you come across that line—didn't want you over here. . . . They turned them back by the hundreds—people that had no proof that they had a job."[114]

Even those who had the right credentials were carefully inspected for insect pests such as boll weevils, bedbugs, and fleas. Any sign of such infestation could mean denial. As Hattye Shields recalled, the border guards were suspicious and unwelcoming, and the time-consuming searches created long traffic backups: "There were cars lined up like you wouldn't believe. . . . Anyone that was carrying any goods at all, any household goods or anything, was pulled over and just really checked thoroughly. . . . My family looked fairly healthy, so there wasn't a long wait for us, but it was just the manner in which they conducted the inspection."[115]

Hard Times Continue

Once past the border, many migrants found that life in California was indeed better than back in the dust bowl. Opportunities were there for those who wanted to work. And, although they were still poor, they had the chance of a better life ahead. "Everyone was good to us," remembered Viola Mitchell. "We lived up there on the hill and every day I bathed the kids and cleaned them up and people seemed to really admire me for it. . . . The people that owned the lease . . . always gave [my husband] Truman work and, my goodness, we thought we was really something."[116]

Others were not as fortunate. Jobs in agriculture were not as easy to get as many had

Okies

Dust bowl migrants faced widespread prejudice in California, and the derogatory term "Okie" expressed the widespread contempt and condescension. A description of the discrimination many faced is included in T.H. Watkins, *The Hungry Years: A Narrative History of the Great Depression in America.*

"Though most had come from Missouri, Arkansas, Texas, Kansas, and Oklahoma, once they made it to California, they usually were lumped together simply as 'Okies.' It was not a term of endearment. . . .

Many residents—particularly those in agricultural areas—heaped contempt upon the outsiders in the time-honored fashion of most human societies, so much so that Okies often competed with Mexican Americans as favorite targets of bigotry. The migrants were 'shiftless trash who live like hogs,' one doctor in Visalia commented, while another was a little kinder when he said, 'There is nothing especially wicked about them—it's just the way they live. There is such a thing as a breed of people. These people have lived separate for too long, and they are like a different race.' They were, a schoolteacher said, 'Adult Children.'"

thought, and wages were extremely low. Many families had to continue their migrant lifestyle, continually moving up and down the state, picking cotton, peas, oranges, or whatever crop was ripe at a certain season. And, with no extra money, they were forced to live under the poorest conditions. "We lived under a tree," recalled Hazel Smalling, who was a young mother at the time. "We just camped right out in the open. [When it rained] we got wet or camped out in the car."[117]

Many clustered together for companionship and protection, forming tent cities along a stream or irrigation ditch that could be used as a source of water. They lived in tiny tents or shacks built of cardboard, scraps of tin, and wood, and ate whatever they could find leftover in the fields. Sometimes that was only green onions. Because the ditches were used for toilets as well as for washing and cooking, water-borne illnesses soon cropped up. So did other diseases. People suffered from boils, intestinal flu, typhus, diphtheria, meningitis, and tuberculosis.

Malnutrition was a problem as well, especially among the children "[I saw] starvation, malnutrition, and profound ignorance of proper hygiene habits," said Doctor Juliet Thorner, who worked at Kern General Hospital in the 1930s and treated many migrant families. "They brought with them many of the customs that had been handed down from generations."[118]

"We Can Speak for Them"

Photographer Dorothea Lange captured the humanity and the desperation of the migrant workers after being hired in 1935 by the California State Emergency Relief Administration to document conditions in labor camps throughout the state.

Lange, born in Hoboken, New Jersey, in 1895, suffered from polio as a child, and the limp she suffered from all her life made her sensitive to the sufferings of others. Her low-profile approach to her work allowed her to get photos that others might have missed, too, and the thoughtfulness she put into her pictures made her work extraordinarily moving. Lange believed that a photographer had a duty to "speak more than of our subjects—we

A dust bowl family relaxes in their makeshift shelter. Many migrants were forced to live in such temporary housing as they moved up and down California looking for work.

can speak with them; we can more than speak about our subjects—we can speak for them."[119] As a result, her photos of sharecroppers, the unemployed, and other victims of the Great Depression served as social documents that revealed their plight to a sometimes uncaring nation.

One of Lange's most poignant photos is titled *Migrant Mother.* In it, a worried young woman sits with one hand to her mouth, her children hiding their faces in her neck. The picture expresses the woman's pride and dignity as well as her hopelessness and despair. Lange, who never posed her subjects for photos, observed, "She [the mother] said that they had been living on frozen vegetables from the surrounding fields, and birds that

the children killed. There she sat in that lean-to tent with her children huddled around her, and seemed to know that my pictures might help her, and so she helped me."[120]

Little by Little

In 1937, the Farm Security Administration began to aid the poorest migrants by building camps in California where they could live in dignity and safety. The camps were set up with small tents or cabins, a common area where women could wash clothes, a well-baby clinic to provide vaccines and check-ups for small children, and a recreation hall. By 1940, there were twelve camps in California

Photographer Dorothea Lange took this photo of a migrant mother and her two children entitled Migrant Mother.

Mixed Blessing

Although the federal government aimed to help those in need, results were often unsatisfactory to farmers like "Bud," whose story is told in Paul Bonnifield's *The Dust Bowl: Men, Dirt, and Depression.*

"A young Morton County, Kansas, farmer set out to follow in his father's footsteps as an honest tiller of the soil. To get started, Bud leased a small place east of Elkhart, Kansas, and borrowed some money from the Federal Land Bank to purchase a team of horses, a few milk cows, and some chickens. He and his family struggled through the early years of the depression . . . [but] the debt could not be paid. When the Resettlement Administration was making its first large land purchases in Morton County in 1935, the Federal Land Bank foreclosed on Bud. . . . The federal government took all but twenty dollars of the gross receipts, as well as his team of horses, cows, and chickens. . . .

Left with twenty dollars, Bud moved his family to Tulsa, Oklahoma, where he lived with a brother for a year without finding steady employment. In 1936 he moved the family back to Elkhart, where he worked at various jobs and on relief [welfare] projects. For Bud the depression and the government foreclosure and land purchase left a bitter memory. His dream for a better tomorrow died in 1936 and there was nothing to replace it except despair. The relief work did, however, play a major role in Bud's ability to care for his family after his return from Tulsa. The story of the young farmer represents the mixed blessing of government relief and land-use planning experienced by many people in the dust bowl."

and several others in other states. Vergie Risner and her family from Oklahoma stayed in the Arvin Federal Government Camp near Lamont, California. "We had two tin cabins. One was used for a bedroom and one for a kitchen. Boy I thought we had a mansion. We got orange crates and put them up for cabinets. We had a Kerosene stove and the House Inspector came by at least once a month."[121]

Over a period of years, the thousands of migrants who were first despised by native Californians for their poverty, backwardness, and shabby appearance eventually blended into the society. They worked hard, sent their children to school, bought homes, and added their customs and traditions to the mix of people already in California. Frank Manies remembered, "Gradually, little by little, after nine years I began to be invited to be a member of all those organizations [Lions Club, Kiwanis Club, Masonic Lodge]. I was a member of the Chamber of Commerce—I was president of the Chamber of Commerce for several years. After nine or ten years I was asked to be a part of the Public Utility District."[122]

The troubles faced by Manies and other migrants taught a valuable lesson, however. There was no Garden of Eden where all of life's problems would vanish, even though some unscrupulous individuals tried to push that belief—for example, promoters who lured migrants to California with promises of work. In fact, farm owners sponsored the promoters and paid the migrants extremely low wages. Joyce Seabolt recalled, "There was a great circulation of leaflets and circulars with glorious offers of jobs in California. . . . What they were trying to do was encourage people to come to California to work as laborers, quite cheap labor, I might add."[123]

Fortunately, those who sincerely wanted to alleviate suffering outnumbered the con men and crooks. One of the concerned, President Franklin Roosevelt, praised the efforts of others who did what they could to improve conditions both in the dust bowl and for migrants in California:

I have been deeply impressed with the general efficiency of those agencies of the Federal, state and local governments which have moved in on the immediate task created by the drought. . . . With this fine help we are tiding over the present emergency. We are going to conserve soil, conserve water and conserve life. We are going to have long-time defenses against both low prices and drought. We are going to have a farm policy that will serve the national welfare. That is our hope for the future.[124]

To Help or Hinder

Conditions in the dust bowl motivated a wide variety of responses from Americans. Ministers, politicians, and other "ordinary folk" tried to lighten the load of those who suffered. Crooks and con men tried to take advantage of people for their own profit. Most discovered that Great Plains families were smart, wary, and hesitant to accept charity except under the most desperate circumstances. As Donald Worster notes, "To ask for aid implied personal and providential [divine] failure. . . . In any case, there was little charity to be had, at least locally: no effective organization to give it out, public or private, in most counties; and nothing to give."[125]

Relying on the Lord

Farm families were self-sufficient, but also deeply religious and had no difficulty turning to God for help in time of trouble. Drought and dust qualified as serious trouble, and in churches throughout the dust bowl, ministers prayed regularly for rain.

Their congregations prayed as well. "Prayer bands"—groups of people willing to pray—were formed throughout Kansas, and some churches held daily prayer meetings for the faithful. In Elkhart, Kansas, in March 1936, a mass prayer meeting was held on the main street of town, and all merchants closed their businesses out of respect for the occasion. A newspaper editor in the town wrote, "Regardless of church affiliation we are all worshipping the same God and let us unite in one earnest appeal to Him for relief."[126]

Some people believed that God was trying to teach his people lessons through the hard times. A few stood on street corners proclaiming that "the storms were the fulfillment of the signs of the times and heralded the approach of the end of the world."[127] Most church members agreed that the world was full of evil and that God would be justified in bringing it to an end. They could not understand, however, why He would single them out when people living in big cities in the eastern United States were just as deserving of punishment. But, as one minister in Hooker, Oklahoma, stated, most Christians felt that "the Lord had put them there [in the dust bowl] for a reason, and it was their obligation to remain."[128]

For whatever reason—insurance, guidance, or comfort—congregations rededicated themselves to God and to living more godly lives, and church attendance grew in dust bowl regions during the 1930s.

The New Deal

While dust bowl residents prayed for rain, the federal government took steps to ease the effects of the Great Depression that caused widespread hardship. Like the farmers in the Great Plains, millions of people in cities and towns from east to west were out of work, had lost their homes, and were facing destitution.

Franklin Delano Roosevelt, elected president in 1932, promised a "new deal" to lead the nation out of the depression, and he pushed Congress to pass laws and reforms that would help those in greatest need. Some of the most well-known agencies created to carry out these reforms were the Civilian Conservation Corps, which provided jobs for the unemployed; the Works Progress Administration, which provided work on public works projects for needy persons; and the Social Security Administration, which provided economic benefits for the unemployed and retirees.

Roosevelt knew that the plains farmers were among the hardest hit by the depression, and some agencies were created specifically to help them. The Department of Agriculture had been formed in 1862 to provide information to farmers about growing crops, but Congress also formed the Agricultural Adjustment Administration in 1933 to regulate farm production as well as to advise and assist farmers during the depression. The

A menacing dust storm approaches a farm. Some dust bowl residents believed the extreme drought and dust to be punishments from God.

Farm Credit Administration made short- and long-term credit available. The Drought Cattle Purchase program paid ranchers for their cattle when they could not sell them at market.

No government-led effort was made to actually stop the blowing dust until 1935, when the Soil Conservation Service was formed. Then, early in 1936, at the request of a group of soil experts from the affected states, 2 million federal dollars were set aside for soil conservation projects. In September of that year, Roosevelt made an inspection tour of the worst-hit areas. Shocked by the poverty and ruin, he pledged more help for the victims. He told the nation in one of his regular "fireside chat" addresses:

I would not have you think for a single minute that there is permanent disaster in these drought regions. . . . No cracked earth, no blistering sun, no burning wind, no grasshoppers, are a permanent match for the indomitable American farmers and stockmen and their wives and children who have carried on through desperate days, and inspire us with their self-reliance, their tenacity and their courage. It was their fathers' task to make homes; it is their task to keep those homes; it is our task to help them with their fight.[129]

Determined to help, Roosevelt listened to what experts and farmers were saying needed to be done in the dust bowl, and then he took action. Families in greatest need were slated to receive federal relief checks and also credit to buy equipment and fuel so they could cultivate their fields properly. The federal government also began purchasing severely damaged land, retiring it from cultivation, and restoring it. State governments were encouraged to adjust tax laws to help

The CCC

The New Deal's Civilian Conservation Corps (CCC) provided job opportunities to many young farmers who welcomed the chance to support their families. As Terry Clipper notes in Oral History Interviews sponsored by the California State University at Bakersfield, California, and accessed on the university library's website (www.lib.csub.edu), the agency also gave some an opportunity to travel.

"In 1935 they had three CCC (Civilian Conservation Corps) which was about fourteen miles from where I lived. . . . So I went in the CCC and got $30. They sent $25 home to my folks and I got to keep $5. . . . That was the greatest thing that ever happened except the WPA [Works Progress Administration]. When President Roosevelt came in and started creating jobs and providing jobs for people that were destitute. I mean good, hard working people with no jobs, no work, nothing.

I went in on June 18 in Ardmore and on January 11, 1936 they moved the whole company to the Grand Canyon in Arizona. . . . We stayed until May 28. While we were there we built fences, roads and landscaped some roads and built some telephone lines. Twice while I was there I walked down to the Colorado River and from this Indian Watch Tower you could see the Colorado River down there. . . . I walked down there twice and that was enough for me."

farmers and also to zone land so farming would be reduced in areas not suitable for agriculture. Communities and individuals were encouraged to follow conservation practices and to work to eliminate erosion on each farm.

Farmers were caught in a difficult situation. They desperately needed aid and would accept government relief only as a last resort. Historian Donald Worster explains: "'Relief' was, by and large, a positive word; it implied a . . . comforting of those overwhelmed by powerful enemies, it meant rushing in reinforcements for those on the front line of battle. To be relieved was an honor, in fact, for no one questioned that you had done your duty well and now deserved a break."[130] From 1933 to 1937, government relief payments provided many dust bowl farmers with their only source of income.

Farmers were also willing to plow under crops and sell their extra cattle and hogs to the government in order to stabilize farm prices. Nevertheless, it seemed a terrible waste to destroy wheat and animals when millions of people were starving. "He [Roosevelt] killed the cattle by the thousands," recalled Robert Dinwiddie. "They [government agents] pitched them over in the big gullies and had them cut open and poured coating all over them so nobody could eat them. That was the President of the United States having that done. Now you can call that a sensible man if you want to but I say if there ever was a crazy man in there he was one of them."[131] In later years, the government allowed those in need to take all the meat they wanted, thus eliminating such reckless waste.

Resettled

The government's land purchase program, run by the federal Resettlement Administra-tion, was controversial as well. The intentions of the programs were good. Small, dusty farms would be purchased and turned back into grazing land. Those who lived on them—usually poor families—would be relocated to land where they could make a better living.

Despite good intentions, the agency seemed to hurt those who were most in need of assistance. It usually offered to pay a minimal price—sometimes less than three dollars an acre—for land that had once been worth ten times that. Many farmers were willing to sell their homesteads, but could not afford to sell at such low prices. They also felt cheated by the low offers. Ann Marie Low's uncle was an example: "For years [my uncle] Grover has been building up his own ranch on land he bought at Arrowwood Lake, a place he calls Pelican Roost. He is offered $15 an acre for it. He paid $25 and hasn't been able to pay it all off. He will come out of the deal in debt for land he no longer has."[132] Grover eventually sold, but other farmers rejected the government's offer, preferring to remain on their property until better times returned.

For those who sold to the government, complications sometimes followed. Because of red tape, payments were slow, leaving families in limbo. Low wrote, "[Our neighbor] Arnold Friedman was furious about the deal he got. . . . All the government would give for the house, the other good buildings, and a quarter-section of land was fifty-six hundred dollars. The land acquisition agent promised the money in the fall, so Arnold sold the horses and machinery. The money still hadn't come. He had no equipment to put in a crop, no money with which to move—nothing."[133]

There were other problems, too. Some families were given no aid. Some families were moved to another county or another state, but given land that was unsuitable for living or farming. Others were given plots of

President Franklin Delano Roosevelt greets farmers in Oklahoma. Roosevelt's New Deal programs helped many dust bowl farmers survive the 1930s.

land too small to farm and told to find other work as well.

Community Action

Roosevelt's New Deal programs helped many people survive the 1930s. Because the government put the good of the national economy over the well-being of individual people, however, the federal aid was not fully appre-ciated. Many in the dust bowl could not decide if it hurt more than it helped.

Unlike government aid, aid from private sources was always a blessing. For instance, customers were grateful when local business owners accepted food or labor instead of cash for their services and allowed customers to buy on credit when money was tight. Hundreds of people appreciated the American Red Cross, which distributed thousands of dust masks and coordinated emergency health care activities. In some locales the agency granted money to help families dust-proof their homes. It also opened six emergency hospitals in Colorado, Kansas, and Texas.

There was also wholehearted support when a community stepped in to avert serious calamity for one of its own, especially when a bank or agency foreclosed on a farm and put it up for sale at auction. Neighbors often congregated at these auctions and used threats against the auctioneer to ensure that prices were kept extremely low. The neighbors then purchased the property for pennies and returned it to the owner. These occasions were dubbed "penny auctions."

One example of such a penny auction involved a Nebraska widow named Theresa Von Baum, who had been unable to pay her mortgage after her husband died. On the day the property was to be sold, over two thousand townspeople surrounded the auction agent and informed him that they did not intend for the widow to be driven off her land. The intimidated agent allowed each of Von Baum's ten cows to be sold for only thirty-five cents, the twenty-four pigs for seventy-five cents, the six horses for $5.60, and the hay binder, corn planter, and disc plow for twenty-five cents apiece. The newly purchased animals and equipment were then given back to the widow, and a quick collection of funds among

During a penny auction of a foreclosed farm, local farmers hang a noose in front of the barn as a warning to the auctioneer not to drive up the price of the property.

the crowd produced $101.02, which was handed over to the auction agent as payment in full for the farm itself. Not willing to oppose such a large crowd, the agent accepted the money and left the premises.

No banker or auction agent was ever injured during numerous penny auctions on the plains, but farmers took action if they had to. A court clerk remembered the day that an unwise bidder actually offered one hundred dollars for a farm that was up for sale. "There was a single moment, then above the massed heads the kicking body of [the] man rose in the room, his arms and legs squirming. . . . They handed him upon solid outstretched arms to the door, and he was emitted [carried out] on a solid band of lifted horny [calloused] hands down the stairs, and I do not know what became of him after that."[134]

Looking Out for Number One

Despite unselfish acts, not everyone was selfless and sacrificing. For instance, suitcase farmers often let their fields erode and blow, even if that made it impossible for their neighbors to preserve their own land.

Some landowners did not honor government agreements, which paid them for not planting their fields on the condition that they not evict renters and sharecroppers on their property. Tenants ate up some of the landowner's profits, however, and were not as efficient as a tractor or a combine. Thus, owners often turned out tenants and invested government money in machinery instead. "In '34 I had I reckon four renters and I didn't make anything. I bought tractors on the money the government give me and got shet [rid] o' my renters,"[135] admitted one man.

Creditors and collection agents were sometimes difficult to deal with, too. Their job was to collect back payments on loans, and some of them did not intend to fail. Some waited at a family's mailbox until government relief checks arrived and then confiscated them. Some—usually those who represented large tractor and combine companies like John Deere or J.I. Case—used high-pressure tactics, including verbal threats and physical violence, when farmers resisted.

Sometimes their intimidation worked. At other times, it backfired. For instance, in Dallam County, Texas, one collector became the target of a farmer's shotgun. Another collector was chased off by a farmer brandishing a razor. A third had his ear bitten off when he got into a fight with a debtor.

Moonshiners

Such violence was rare and spontaneous, and those who carried it out were otherwise law-abiding citizens. So were many dust bowl bootleggers who produced and marketed illegal liquor while Prohibition was law between 1920 and 1933. Clarence Graham remembered,

> I know of one man . . . named Bible. He was a very fine, good man. He was an honest, upright man. I don't think he drank. I don't think he smoked. . . . He was in financial straits, so he started moonshining. They finally caught him and took him to jail. He said, "Well, I've got my farm paid off now. . . . I was in debt so bad, that if I hadn't done this I was going to lose my farm."[136]

Like so many other people who broke the Constitution's Eighteenth Amendment, which made producing, transporting, and selling liquor illegal in the 1920s, farmers trying to

"Pretty Boy" Floyd used some of the money he robbed from banks to help needy dust bowl families.

contributed to the deaths of many people because of the poison and impurities it contained. Local law enforcers were inclined to overlook this kind of lawbreaking, however. Many did not support Prohibition. Others understood the desperation that drove moonshiners to break the law. Thus, when local police came upon a still, they usually destroyed it but did not try to arrest the owner. Moonshiners who were actually arrested usually received light sentences from a sympathetic judge.

Dust Bowl Killers

Bootleggers and moonshiners were tolerated in the dust bowl, but other lawbreakers caused more harm and were hunted by law enforcement agents with ruthlessness and determination. One of these was Charles Arthur Floyd, known as "Pretty Boy" Floyd, a bank robber and murderer who grew up in the Cookson Hills of Oklahoma. Born in 1904, he earned his nickname in 1925 when a witness to one of his robberies described him as "a mere boy—a pretty boy with apple cheeks."[137]

Floyd was a killer, but during the 1930s he also distinguished himself by tearing up farm mortgages that were held in bank vaults that he robbed in Oklahoma. He also used some of his money to help those most in need. Jeffery S. King, who wrote *The Life and Death of Pretty Boy Floyd*, states, "He was generous to kids and old people. . . . It was reported he was feeding a dozen families."[138] Because of his generous deeds, folks in Cookson Hills began calling Floyd the "Robin Hood of Oklahoma." Some farm families in the region risked their lives to hide him from authorities. By June 1934, however, Floyd's many crimes put him at the top of the Public Enemies List of J. Edgar Hoover, director of

scratch out a living for their families often sold corn to moonshiners (illegal liquor manufacturers). Some, like Bible, even set up a still and made moonshine whiskey themselves. In the early 1930s, nearly fifty thousand gallons of "white lightning" (whiskey) was produced and sold every week in a five-county region that supplied whiskey for the cities of Denver and Dallas.

The liquor trade was illegal, and helped promote organized crime. Moonshine also

A Tasteless Public Display

The death of Bonnie and Clyde sparked excitement among dust bowl residents and other Americans who were looking for distractions from poverty and hard times. Thousands of curiosity-seekers flocked to see their bodies, as Bonnie's mother, Emma Parker, remembers in her book, *The True Story of Bonnie and Clyde*. An excerpt from the book can be found on the Internet at the Cinetropic website (www.cinetropic.com).

"When the bodies arrived in Dallas on the morning of May 24, [1934] people behaved in about the same manner as they did in Arcadia, [Louisiana, where the couple was killed] but the Dallas police made an effort to control them. Twenty thousand people jammed the street in front of the funeral home where Bonnie lay and almost as many came to view Clyde. It was a Roman holiday. Hot dog stands were set up; soda pop vendors arrived to serve those who waited to view all that was left of the South's most noted desperadoes.

The final grim and sardonic touch was the great loads of flowers that arrived. It was impossible to hold the crowds back and they were wrecking both the place where Bonnie lay and the establishment where Clyde had been taken. Some newsboys contributed money for wreaths for Clyde and Bonnie. A small bouquet of lilies arrived with a note asking that they be placed in Bonnie's hands that night. The sender said that another bouquet would be sent the following day when these flowers had wilted, and asked that the wilted bunch be saved and given to me. I don't know who the person was."

The exploits of gangsters like Bonnie Parker and Clyde Barrow provided many dust bowl farmers with a welcome distraction from their difficulties.

the Federal Bureau of Investigation (FBI). FBI sharpshooters killed Floyd on October 22 of that year, and more than twenty thousand admirers attended his funeral. Biographer Joseph Geringer writes, "Less a bad man than a symbol of a turbulent era in the saga of the sagebrush, . . . he is remembered in legend and in song, recalled not with a shudder but with almost a fond salute."[139]

Other dust bowl killers who made Hoover's Public Enemies List were Clyde Barrow and his girlfriend Bonnie Parker. They gained a reputation for shooting state troopers and robbing banks in Texas, Oklahoma, Missouri, Louisiana, and New Mexico beginning in 1932. Both Bonnie and Clyde came from dirt-poor Texas families. Both were angry at life and the government for allowing the Great Depression to beat the "little guy" down even further than he had been before. Although they terrorized bank tellers and store owners and were responsible for several murders, Americans in the 1930s were thrilled to hear about their adventures. When the couple was gunned down on May 23, 1934, near Shreveport, Louisiana, many mourned their deaths. Historian Jonathan Davis explained that, in a time when even law-abiding people were angry with the government, Bonnie and Clyde were heroes. "Anybody who robbed banks or fought the law [was] really living out some secret fantasies [of] a large part of the public,"[140] Davis stated.

The Rainmakers

Rainmakers who began appearing in towns as the drought lengthened were less notorious than Pretty Boy Floyd and Bonnie and Clyde, but just as unconventional when it came to careers. Many were out to make a fast dollar

by taking advantage of the naive. Others sincerely believed in their ability to break the drought. While most dust bowl residents were skeptical, the rainmakers gave everyone something to talk about and brought hope to those who were desperate enough to try anything.

The most popular and widely used approach to opening the clouds had always involved the use of explosives. From early times, people in war noticed that it often rained heavily after a battle. Rainstorms were also linked to thunder, a natural concussion. Thus when explosives expert Ward A. "Tex" Thornton, known as the "king of the oil well fire fighters," decided to try to make it rain in 1935, he relied on explosives to do the trick. Thornton's plan was simple: He persuaded Texas farmers and ranchers to pay him three-hundred dollars for TNT and nitroglycerin, which he planned to attach to balloons on strings. The explosives would be set to go off at twenty-minute intervals and would float high into the sky via the balloons.

Thornton set up his experiment near Dalhart, Texas, on May 1, 1935. Several thousand ranchers, farmers, reporters, and photographers gathered to watch, but had to take cover when a sudden dust storm blew up. Thornton realized that, due to the wind, he could not send the balloons aloft, so he compromised by burying the explosives in the ground. The blasts that followed sent dirt high into the air, where it mixed with the blowing dust and pelted onlookers. No rain was produced, however. The drought went on. The dust continued to blow.

There were others like Thornton who were sincere in their belief that explosions led to rain, and it was natural that at least some of them would share their suggestions for a remedy for drought. One Texas man sent a telegram to President Roosevelt asking

Mr. Post

Two decades before rainmakers appeared in the dust bowl in the 1930s, cereal magnate C.W. Post tried rainmaking to save his crops in Texas. Post financed several "rain battles" that he was convinced would produce healthy downpours. Two of these battles are described in Vance Johnson's *Heaven's Tableland: The Dust Bowl Story*.

"The first battle was staged between 4:05 and 5:03 PM on the afternoon of June 8, 1911. A total of 171 charges of dynamite, each containing two pounds, was fired—as nearly in unison as possible. Great handfuls of earth and rock were thrown into the air. The explosions rattled the windows in Post City several miles away. But no rain fell. . . .

[Another] big-scale battle was 'fought' on the afternoon of August 23. Altogether, fifteen hundred two-pound charges were fired, and [Post's field commander A.D.] Marhoff was proud of the precision achieved by his men. That night more than an inch of rain soaked the Post lands.

Post was overjoyed. 'I believe we have reason to feel we have demonstrated that firing these charges in large numbers, and scattered on an area of one or two miles, will really produce rain,' he wrote his managers. . . .

Unfortunately for Post's rain-making theory . . . the rain which fell the night after the August 23 bombardment was just the beginning of a rainy spell. . . . Post, a careful man with his money, decided to wait until a rain was needed before exploding any more dynamite."

him to declare a national "Explosion Day," during which every county in the United States would fire off explosives at the same time. An Ohio man suggested a "radio rainmaker"—a recording of a severe thunderstorm that would be played over a powerful amplifying system. A prominent Kansas City lawyer begged Secretary of Agriculture Henry A. Wallace to "lend" him a hundred pieces of field artillery so that he could set them off and make rain.

Most dust bowl residents had little time to waste on rainmakers' theories. They were too busy fighting to survive until better times came. Eventually, their efforts and endurance were rewarded. Slowly, in more and more places, the drought began to end. Rain began to fall toward the end of the decade, raising spirits while it dampened the fields. Melt White remembered the hope it brought to many: "There'd be lightning back in the Northwest, you'd see flickering lightning and Dad would say, 'That'll be in here about 2 o'clock in the morning.' But the rain was so welcome and [it] smelt so good I'd lay and listen to [the raindrops] pitter patter on the side of the old house at night and we'd really sleep. Cause it was a wonderful feeling."[141]

The Dust Settles

Despite antigovernment feelings, criminals, and confusion, slow changes for the better took place in the dust bowl as 1940 approached. Some changes were due to rain. Some were due to government aid. Some were due to farmers putting into practice techniques that saved water and kept the soil in place. J.R. Davison remembered, "During those Dirty Thirties they came out with a lot of these different methods—contour farming, you know, different things, summer puddling. . . . You pulled a little apparatus behind your plow that just dug holes and that'd catch that water. You know, you could have a two- or three-inch rain and it wouldn't run off."[142]

Adapting to New Ideas

Most of the new farming practices introduced in the 1930s were based on practicality. For instance, plowing using a lister heaped dirt on both sides of the furrow to trap more drifting soil; it also buried fine soil particles and brought up larger, heavier ones. Contour plowing, in which farmers followed the natural shape of the field as opposed to creating straight furrows, formed small dams to catch moisture. Puddling—digging small pits to catch water when it fell—reduced water runoff as well. Rough tillage, which left stubble in the fields during fallow (resting) periods, held down soil. Allowing a field to lie fallow every other year improved its fertility as

well. Strip planting, which alternated strips of wheat with wind-resistant, drought-resistant crops such as sorghum or small grains, stabilized soil, too.

Convincing farmers to use the new techniques was not always easy. J.R. Davison noted: "They [the government] came out with a lot of these methods, but most of these old-timers wouldn't do it. . . . Finally they got where they'd pay 'em. You know, you could make a dollar an acre if you practiced one of these methods. And that got a lot of 'em workin' on it because they needed that dollar an acre during those days."[143] Even with financial incentives, not all farmers cooperated. Donald Worster notes, "It was not something they were used to. Most of them were used, for example, to plowing in straight lines and that was a very aesthetically [artistically] appealing idea. Still is. I mean, you can fly over the country and still see people who love that straight line regardless of the slope."[144]

Some farmers hesitated to spend their hard-earned money on equipment such as duck-foot cultivators, which sheared off surface weeds without deep plowing. Some complained that they could not afford to let land lie fallow when they needed all the crops they could raise and sell. Worster notes that the new farming practices "were costly, they were complicated, they required technical skills. In some cases, they might seem to inhibit production. Government itself waxed and waned in terms of its enthusiasm for supporting them. So it's never been a process of simply

A Pueblo, Colorado, street is flooded after a rainstorm. Beginning in 1938, a series of rainstorms offered relief to dust bowl states.

converting overnight into good soil conservation techniques."[145]

Help from Ecologists

Experts like the Department of Agriculture's Hugh Hammond Bennett, the first director of the Soil Conservation Service, encouraged and aided farmers in their conservation efforts. Bennett was instrumental in getting a large commitment of federal money to fight the dust. "If we are bold in our thinking, courageous in accepting new ideas, and willing to work *with* instead of *against* our land,

we shall find in conservation farming an avenue of the greatest food production the world has ever known,"[146] he stated.

Ecologists like Charles Whitfield, also of the Soil Conservation Service, were in a more hands-on position than Bennett. In 1936, Whitfield was assigned the task of reclaiming some damaged farmland near Dalhart, Texas. Although the land had been farmed for only three years, it was almost totally stripped of life. Huge sand dunes, some thirty-six feet high, covered what had once been fields. Wind continued to shift the dunes, and the air was filled with blowing sand. "The wind built these dunes," Whitfield observed to his work crew. "The wind will tear them down. We are going to make the wind work for us, not against us, for a change."[147] Using wood and sheet metal to form solid fencelike barriers he called "wind intensifiers," Whitfield began to direct the movement of the blowing sand so it blew down slopes to fill in low spots. In eighteen months, he slowly decreased the height of the dunes, reducing one thirty-six-foot-high mound to a height lower than an automobile. Over the same period, he began planting new drought-resistant African grain crops— Sudan grass, Kafir corn, Hegari sorghum, and others—that would begin to hold the soil in place. After that grain grew and was harvested, he left the stubble in the ground to provide further erosion control.

Soaking Rain

Whitfield was only one of several ecologists who worked out methods of restoring land in the dust bowl. Their work was made easier by the easing of the drought in 1938 and 1939. On a trip through the plains states, President Roosevelt made a quick stop in Amarillo, Texas, on July 11, 1938, and made a speech while rain drenched both him and his entourage. "If I had asked the newspapermen on the train what the odds were, they would have given me 100 to 1 that it wouldn't be raining in Amarillo. But it is!"[148] he told a cheering crowd.

Rain was sporadic and the dust continued to blow, but well-timed precipitation was starting to help crops grow. The progress was heartening. In the *Ochiltree County Herald* (Perryton, Texas) on January 12, 1939, headlines read, "Slow Downpour Lets Every Drop Soak into Ground; Is Followed By Spring Weather—Moisture During 1938 Was Above Normal." The *Elkhart* [Kansas] *Tri-State*

News on March 31 read, "Wettest Season in Years. . . . A soaking spring rain falling all night Tuesday put the final touches on the old time dust bowl," and headlines in the April 6 *Stratford* [Texas] *Star* proclaimed, "Heavy Rains Insure Harvest of Large Yield of Wheat."[149]

Farmers who had not harvested crops since 1932 did so in 1939. As early as 1938, the Texas panhandle produced 18 million bushels of wheat, and in the Oklahoma panhandle, two-thirds of the wheat that was planted was harvested. Good-size regions in western Kansas and Colorado had weed or crop cover for the first time since 1933. "It was a very emotional time, when you'd get rain, because it meant so much to you. You didn't have false hope then," said Floyd Coen of Kansas. "When the rain came, it meant life itself. It meant a future."[150]

Change in Government

By 1941, drought in the plains was a thing of the past. Rain fell, crops grew, farmers brought in good harvests, and life returned to normal. Nevertheless, the dust bowl was not forgotten. It had produced too much lasting and significant change in the government, in the economy, and among those who experienced its hardships firsthand.

One of the greatest changes came in the federal government's approach to running the country. Before the 1930s, the government had remained uninvolved in farm practices, favoring state and local management. President Herbert Hoover had supported some measures to help farmers, but these mainly focused on state programs and relief from charitable organizations like the Red Cross. "Hoover liked to have starved us all to death. It was rough when he got in in 1928, but he only served one term," remembered James

Lackey. "Then Roosevelt got in and things started picking up."[151]

With the election of Franklin Roosevelt, the federal government began assuming greater responsibility for the economic growth and security of the nation and the people.

When it came to farming, that translated to a system of price supports and subsidies (financial assistance) that helped farmers make profits.

Although some people resented federal policies and spending and made fun of the government's many "alphabet soup agencies,"

The Father of Soil Conservation

Hugh Hammond Bennett was disliked by some farmers who resented his criticism of their farming practices. In "Surviving the Dust Bowl," found on the PBS website (www.pbs.org), producer Chana Gazit points out that Bennett had the good of the country at heart.

"Hugh Hammond Bennett, who would come to be known as 'the father of soil conservation,' had been leading a campaign to reform farming practices with the intention of preserving the soil well before Roosevelt became president. In the mid-1930's desperate Dust Bowl farmers took little solace [comfort] in hearing from Bennett that . . . 'Americans have been the greatest destroyers of land of any race or people, barbaric or civilized.' Further, he went on to call for 'a tremendous national awakening to the need for action in bettering our agricultural practices.' Despite such statements, Bennett was not insensitive to hardships faced by Dust Bowl farmers. Rather,

he urged a new approach to farming in order to avoid similar catastrophes in the future.

In April 1935, Bennett was on his way to testify before a Congressional committee when he learned of a dust storm blowing in from the western plains. At last, he would be able to present tangible evidence of the results of short-sighted farming practices. As a dusty gloom settled over the nation's capital and blotted out the midday sun, Bennett exclaimed, 'This, gentlemen, is what I have been talking about.' Congress responded by passing the Soil Conservation Act of 1935. In turn, the Roosevelt administration put its full weight and authority behind improving farming techniques."

Hugh Hammond Bennett (center) talks with fellow conservationists during a 1930s conference.

The Rain Returns

By 1939, the drought was disappearing and hopes were rising on the Great Plains. On August 8, the following article, included in Paul Bonnifield's book *The Dust Bowl: Men, Dirt, and Depression*, appeared in the *Texhoma* [Oklahoma] *Times*.

"Seven years of choking dust, whipped over the Southwest by restless winds, vainly tried to lick the faith and hope of the people. Many became discouraged when things looked blackest, but kept on hoping and trusting in themselves and in this country. Some left for various reasons. . . . Then came 1939. There were comparatively few dust storms. Rains came and green covered the land. Wheat looked excellent, although hail took some of it. A million bushels came to Texhoma and all this has instilled new hope and courage in the citizens of the high plains. 'Dust Bowl' is a term to be discarded and forgotten. The new term should be 'the land of beautiful sunsets— where the sun rises and sets on the most courageous and friendly folks in America.'"

most soon grew used to having government as a safety net in times of trouble. From the New Deal era on, the U.S. federal government was seen as an agent of social and economic reform, expected to provide some type of assistance—Social Security, farm subsidies, and welfare—to care for those in greatest need.

Because he was the sponsor of all this change, President Roosevelt went down in history as one of America's most controversial commanders in chief. Clara Davis remembered an incident that took place as early as 1932:

I was sitting on the front porch and an elderly man came down the street. He was a friend of my father's and he stopped and talked for a minute. He started to cross the street and a car drove up and a man jumped out and picked up a rock and hit him in the head. . . . The people in the car had hit this elderly man because he had voted for Franklin Roosevelt.[152]

Many people grew more enthusiastic as the president's policies helped the nation recover. "I thought Roosevelt was one of the greatest things that ever was. I still do," recalled Lackey. "I don't know why but that's when we started getting on our feet."[153] Others complained about him and his policies. "Roosevelt was the worst thing that ever happened to the United States of America," stated Oklahoman James Ward. "He started the country on a spending spree and it snowballed."[154]

Other Changes

At the end of the 1930s, not only was there more government involvement in farming, but there was a new feel about farming on the plains. Small "substandard" farms had been eliminated. Larger, more efficient farms were becoming typical of the region. Farming was also becoming more of a business than a way of life. People worked their land with modern machines rather than a horse and plow, putting the emphasis on large profits rather than self-sufficiency. "[The farmer in Haskell County, Kansas] believes himself to be as much a businessman as a manufacturer is,"[155] stated Earl Bell of the Bureau of Agricultural Economics in 1942.

Along with a change in farm size and practices, the dust bowl opened the eyes of the nation to the issue of ecology. Many people who had ignored the abuse of the land in the past realized that enormous economic and social repercussions would result if humans did not focus on water and land conservation, air pollution, species survival, and other conservation measures.

While some people were interested in preserving the earth for future generations, most people on the Great Plains were concerned with conservation as it related directly to farming. Their goal was to preserve the land so they could grow crops and make money. To that end, most states established soil conservation districts, locally run groups of farmers who were interested in implementing new

The First Lady Comes to Town

First Lady Eleanor Roosevelt was as politically active as her husband and often represented him on various trips throughout the country. Herman Lawson remembers, in an interview with the author, one momentous occasion when she visited his hometown of Bristow, Oklahoma.

"My Dad never discussed politics with anyone because he was a Republican. He did not like President Roosevelt, but he did approve some of his efforts to help the poor and hungry through the WPA [Works Progress Administration] and other federal programs. . . .

Eleanor Roosevelt came to Bristow to give a 4th of July speech one year. The occasion was held at an outdoor theater with concrete benches lining the hillside. Several

thousand came from near and far. Even my Dad took our family early to grab one of the concrete seats.

During Mrs. Roosevelt's speech a man tripped in the aisle in front of my Dad and bumped into him. 'I'm so sorry,' he said and he continued on down the aisle. A short time later Dad missed his wallet. Several people missed their wallets that day. Pickpockets followed the President's wife around the country practicing their trade. This experience didn't endear the Roosevelts to my Dad."

First Lady Eleanor Roosevelt often represented her husband, President Roosevelt, during visits across the country.

techniques that would save their farms. One-fifth of the dust bowl region was organized into such districts by 1940. Each operated according to the will of local members, and some districts even allowed local farmers to take steps to stop erosion on farms where the landlords were absent or negligent.

Conservation was also advanced through the Shelterbelt Project, begun in 1937 to create windbreaks that would stop blowing soil. Sponsored by Roosevelt himself, the undertaking initially called for large-scale planting of trees stretching in a hundred-mile-wide zone from Canada to northern Texas. Due to costs and other practicalities, the project was scaled back, but farmers were still paid to plant and cultivate native trees such as red cedar and green ash, which were placed along fences separating

Farmers plant a shelterbelt strip of trees in Oklahoma. The Shelterbelt Project called for a hundred-mile-long zone of trees designed to create windbreaks.

properties. In time, 220 million trees were planted on thirty thousand farms, although most were located east of the dust bowl.

From an ecological perspective, the Shelterbelt Project was only a limited success. Its trees would have been more effective if they had been planted in greater numbers west rather than east of the plains. However, farm families quickly realized that the project had personal benefits for them. The addition of greenery was inspiring to those who saw nothing but the level, brown landscape day after day. "When I'm feeling flatter than a pancake and bluer than a whetstone [stone used for sharpening tools], I just go out and walk among those trees," said one woman. "Walking along by those trees and feeling the branches hitting me, and hearing the birds singing—Well, I just can't tell you what that means. For lifting a person's spirit, there's nothing better."[156]

Strong Memories

Government and society had changed by the end of the dust bowl, but so had individuals who had lived with the dust through the "dirty thirties."

Some people were left to cope with health problems. Historian Vance Johnson noted, "Only time could measure the years lopped off the life span of men and women who had eaten dust eight years and had become bent and gray with work and worry."[157] In some regions, doctors found that many people showed spots on their lungs when they had a chest X-ray. The spots did not seem to indicate tuberculosis or any other disease. They were simply remnants of the dust that so many had inhaled.

Most people who lived through the dust bowl were left with memories that would af-

fect them for the rest of their lives. Some of these memories were touching—merry Christmases although there were no gifts; trips to town in an old jalopy; cornbread and milk with family around the dinner table. "My family joked in later years that we lived on beans for seven years,"[158] remembered Herman Lawson.

But people also had grim recollections of discouragement and broken dreams: starving cattle, empty fields, a child's used-up college fund. Marguerite Dunmire, a teacher in the 1930s, was haunted by the words of one of her students, a thin, pale little girl who could not concentrate on her studies. When told to go home, have a snack, and rest, the little girl replied, "Oh, I can't do that. Today is my sister's turn to eat."[159] Other people remembered hostility and discrimination in California. Juanita Price recalled,

> There was what they call a tent city out there at Edison [near Bakersfield]. The people didn't have anything to live off of or build with and they just used cardboard and sacks and rags or whatever to build little shelters to live in. People would go out there and disturb them. It was horrible. There was lots of little children running around out there with half enough clothes. They had dirty noses and sores around their mouths from malnutrition. . . . It wasn't that they deliberately wanted to be filthy. It was that they couldn't help it.[160]

For the rest of their lives, people who lived through the dust bowl followed behavior patterns that stemmed from those years when money was tight and nothing was wasted. "Two things I like now is having money in my billfold," said Earl Butler. "I don't mean $50. I mean $200 to $300 or

Memories of children's sacrifices were especially painful for parents who lived through the dust bowl. In an Oral History Interview sponsored by California State University, Bakersfield, California, accessed on the university library's website www.lib.csub.edu, Lillie May relates a story about her daughter she only learned about years later.

"My daughter was taking dancing lessons and she was good. . . . She was taking piano lessons and was very good at that and all of a sudden her dancing teacher called me up and said, 'Lillie, what's the matter with Shirley? She hasn't been the last three Saturdays.' I said, 'Well, there's been nothing wrong.' . . . I talked to Shirley Ann about it and she said, 'Mother, I decided I would do more on my piano and I'm not going to take dancing anymore.'

Do you know I didn't find out why she quit dancing until after she was married. . . . We were talking and I said, 'Shirley Ann, you would have been a wealthy woman today if you'd stuck with your dancing.' She said, 'Mother, you want to know why I quit dancing? . . . I knew when I broke my ballet slippers you did not have the money to buy me another pair but you would have got it someway or other,' and she said, 'I didn't need it that much.'

I thought 'Well, maybe in a way I was wrong letting my children know the situation we were in, but then when you look at it another way I think it made a better person out of them because they had to make decisions that other kids didn't make.'"

more. Also I still remember the one light, the 40 watt light in the bedroom with all us kids crowded in there trying to read or do our homework, so I like plenty of light."[161] And Rosie Laird said, "I just won't throw nothing away as long as it can be used. Now I [make quilts from] old jeans or [my husband Alvin's] old striped overalls."[162]

New Concerns

The bad memories faded with time, but never entirely disappeared. They were pushed from the forefront, however, by the outbreak of World War II in 1939. That year, Adolf Hitler invaded Poland and then set out to conquer the rest of Europe. Two years later, in December 1941, the United States joined the war after the Japanese bombed the U.S. naval base at Pearl Harbor in Hawaii, destroying eighteen ships and two hundred planes, and taking thousands of lives.

The war revived the depressed U.S. economy. Men and women who had been unemployed throughout the Great Depression quickly found work building ships and manufacturing weapons to use in combat. Millions of soldiers joined the fight. Patriotism and support for the government skyrocketed. The nation was united in wanting to defeat the enemy.

The war brought an end to several dust bowl projects, however. Conservation programs were significantly reduced. Government money set aside for agricultural equipment was channeled to building ships and tanks. Without that aid, some families again went into debt to finance farm improvements. And, with a new demand for food for the troops, some farmers began to slip back into their old ways—planting wheat in more of their fields, grazing too many animals on pastureland, and not allowing land to lie fallow to renew itself.

A few experts watched anxiously and wondered what would happen if the rain stopped again. Most people did not think they would ever have to contemplate such a scenario. "[People seem to be] thinking differently than they did," observed one optimistic farmer in 1936. "It seems like they are interested now in doing something about soil blowing." "Don't fool yourself," replied his friend. "Just wait until we get about two good wheat crops in a row, and good prices. Then see what happens."[163] The answer was unwelcome but true. The character of the plains was the same. It seemed that farmers had not learned their lesson. So the future held the key. Only time would tell if there would be another dust bowl or not.

Another Dust Bowl?

The cost of the dust bowl in terms of human suffering remains untold. The cost in dollars and cents has never been fully calculated either, although experts estimate that it may have reached $1 billion in 1930s dollars. In today's values, that figure would be at least ten times larger.

Most people would agree, however, that all the suffering and the cost are in the past. More important to everyone today is the answer to the question, could the dust bowl happen again?

Yes or No?

Many people say "no." Farmers have learned techniques to protect their fields from wind erosion. They have been able to tap into reservoirs of water deep below the earth's surface and can draw from them to irrigate crops. They have government support to aid them when crops fail or prices are low. The Soil and Water Conservation Society of America claims that modern farming is "the most sustainable in history,"[164] due to high-yield seeds, chemical fertilizers, pest management, and minimal tillage of the soil.

Other people believe that another dust bowl is possible. They cite the carelessness of American farmers who still plant crops on marginal land, who raise too many cattle, and who count on the government to pull them out of a tight spot when times get hard. "We have mainly learned to go to the federal government for relief and to depend on irrigation to save us from drought,"[165] says historian Donald Worster, whose parents fled the dust bowl. He points out that underground water can be depleted during times of drought. Then crops would die and the land would once again be vulnerable to winds.

Experts like Worster also point out that the cycle of drought and heat will continue to repeat itself on the plains. These experts have been proven right once already, in the 1950s. During that decade, rainfall was low, temperatures soared, and the dust blew, although to a lesser extent than in the 1930s. Crop yields in some areas dropped as much as 50 percent. Grasslands were scorched. With grass scarce and hay prices high, some ranchers were once again forced to feed their cattle prickly pear cactus. As one dust bowl resident pointed out, "The government didn't follow the plan of FDR and so our land is still a dustbowl hit by duststorms and the duststorms are getting higher and wilder and meaner, and the hearts of the people are sickly worried. . . . That old dustbowl is still there, and that high dirt-wind is still there. The government didn't fix that and Congress couldn't put a stop to it."[166]

The Greenhouse Effect

Some people believe that the greenhouse effect and global warming may also increase the risk of another dust bowl. The greenhouse effect is the retention of heat at the earth's surface caused by the presence of gases such as water vapor, carbon dioxide, and methane. These gases may produce global warming, an increase in the average temperature of the earth's atmosphere, leading to changes in climate.

No one knows exactly how global warming and the greenhouse effect might affect the Great Plains. Many that contemplate the problem are fearful, however. Donald Worster writes,

There is a very strong possibility that global warming is going to make some areas of the world much wetter, as we are seeing right now, and make other areas much drier. It's going to lead to a new era of extremes. While we cannot predict the exact geography of those patterns, it seems fairly likely that the Great Plains, especially the southern Great Plains, are going to be drier, more drought ridden in the future, hotter in the summers than they have been over the last fifty years since the Great Depression and the Dust Bowl, which means a strong likelihood of more dust storms [and] wind erosion.[167]

In an effort to learn more in order to prevent further tragedies in the Great Plains and elsewhere in the United States, Congress passed the National Drought Policy Act in 1998. The National Drought Policy Commission, created by the new law, determined that the United States had no comprehensive policy to reduce the impact of drought. It recommended taking active steps to prepare for another drought if it happened, so that its effects on the nation could be reduced. The

A Matter of Time

Although no one can predict whether another dust bowl will occur in the future or not, journalist Dave Mowitz notes in an 1999 article titled "History Warns of Another Dust Bowl" that at least two climatologists—experts who study climate—are convinced that one will. Mowitz's article can be found at the *Agriculture Online* website (www.agriculture.com).

"The severe drought that crippled Texas and Oklahoma last summer isn't necessarily a predictor of an impending dry period like that during the 'Dust Bowl' era of the 1930s. But two climatologists are convinced another drought like the Dust Bowl will happen in the future.

Connie Woodhouse and Jonathan Overpeck have been studying natural evidence found in tree rings, archaeological findings and lakebed sediment [and] combining it with historical records. That evidence inspired them to conclude that a severe drought occurs in the Great Plains region once or twice every century. They are, however, less certain when the next such drought will occur.

Woodhouse, who is a climatologist at the University of Colorado, and Overpeck, who is with the National Oceanic and Atmospheric Administration, point out that the Dust Bowl drought wasn't the most severe such event to hit the Great Plains. Evidence indicates that more prolonged droughts hit the western US in the 13th and 16th centuries. Those dry periods lasted approximately 20 years as compared to 8 years for the Dust Bowl and covered a larger geographic area."

A farmer in Oklahoma assesses damage done to his cornfield following a severe drought in 1998. Some experts believe future dust bowl scenarios are very possible.

commission stated, "We must adopt a forward-looking stance to reduce this nation's vulnerability. . . . Preparedness—especially drought planning, plan implementation, and proactive mitigation—must become the cornerstone of national drought policy."[168]

Even with preparedness, no one can rule out for certain the possibility of another dust bowl as severe as that of the 1930s. Douglas Hurt said in 1981, "Another Dust Bowl is not inevitable, but, given the right circumstances, it is possible."[169] If disaster does strike, thousands of courageous, persistent Great Plains residents, like the farmers who remained on their land in the 1930s, will see the disaster through. They will be like Edith Lewis of Elkhart, Kansas, who summed up the resolve and buoyancy of the survivor when she said, "Those were hard times. . . . A lot of people left while the storms were going on, but [my husband] E.P. and I decided to stay. We're glad we did."[170]

Notes

Introduction: Black Blizzards

1. Quoted in R. Douglas Hurt, *The Dust Bowl: An Agricultural and Social History.* Chicago: Nelson-Hall, 1981, p. 1.
2. Quoted in Michael Parfit, "The Dust Bowl," *Smithsonian*, June 1989, p. 44.
3. Quoted in Paul Bonnifield, *The Dust Bowl: Men, Dirt, and Depression.* Albuquerque: University of New Mexico Press, 1979, p. 75.
4. Quoted in Donald Worster, *Dust Bowl: The Southern Plains in the 1930s.* Oxford: Oxford University Press, 1979, p. 28.
5. Quoted in Hurt, *The Dust Bowl*, p. 33.
6. Quoted in PBS Online, "Surviving the Dust Bowl," *The American Experience*, 1999. www.pbs.org.
7. Quoted in Hurt, *The Dust Bowl*, p. 59.
8. Worster, *Dust Bowl*, p. 97.

Chapter 1: The Great Plow-Up

9. T.H. Watkins, *The Hungry Years: A Narrative History of the Great Depression in America.* New York: Henry Holt, 1999, pp. 425–26.
10. Quoted in Hurt, *The Dust Bowl*, p. 4.
11. Quoted in Hurt, *The Dust Bowl*, pp. 4–5.
12. Quoted in Hurt, *The Dust Bowl*, pp. 7–8.
13. Quoted in PBS Online, "Surviving the Dust Bowl."
14. Quoted in Hurt, *The Dust Bowl*, p. 25.
15. Quoted in PBS Online, "Surviving the Dust Bowl."
16. Quoted in Bonnifield, *The Dust Bowl*, p. 40.
17. Quoted in Parfit, "The Dust Bowl," p. 45.
18. Quoted in Vance Johnson, *Heaven's Tableland: The Dust Bowl Story.* New York: Farrar, Straus, 1947, p. 80.
19. Quoted in Johnson, *Heaven's Tableland*, p. 118.
20. Caroline A. Henderson, "Letters from the Dust Bowl," *Atlantic Monthly*, May 1936, p. 546.
21. Quoted in Bonnifield, *The Dust Bowl*, p. 48.
22. Quoted in Lisa Levitt Ryckman, "Plains," *Denver Rocky Mountain News*, March 26, 1999. www.denver-rmn.com.
23. Quoted in Johnson, *Heaven's Tableland*, p. 139.
24. Oral History Interviews, Dust Bowl Migration Digital Archives, California State University Bakersfield Library, 2003. www.lib.csub.edu.
25. Quoted in Peter Jennings and Todd Brewster, *The Century*, New York: Doubleday Dell, 1998, p. 150.
26. Johnson, *Heaven's Tableland*, p. 186.
27. Quoted in PBS Online, "Surviving the Dust Bowl."
28. Quoted in PBS Online, "Surviving the Dust Bowl."

Chapter 2: Life in the Dusters

29. Quoted in PBS Online, "Surviving the Dust Bowl."
30. Ann Marie Low, *Dust Bowl Diary.* Lincoln: University of Nebraska Press, 1984, p. 101.
31. Low, *Dust Bowl Diary*, p. 152.
32. Quoted in PBS Online, "Surviving the Dust Bowl."
33. Quoted in Worster, *Dust Bowl*, p. 17.
34. Low, *Dust Bowl Diary*, pp. 28–29.
35. Oral History Interviews.
36. Low, *Dust Bowl Diary*, p. 97.

37. Quoted in Bonnifield, *The Dust Bowl*, p. 191.
38. Quoted in Worster, *Dust Bowl*, p. 22.
39. Oral History Interviews.
40. Parfit, "The Dust Bowl," p. 50.
41. Quoted in Johnson, *Heaven's Tableland*, pp. 148–49.
42. Oral History Interviews.
43. Quoted in PBS Online, "Surviving the Dust Bowl."
44. Johnson, *Heaven's Tableland*, p. 157.
45. Quoted in Hurt, *The Dust Bowl*, p. 53.
46. Quoted in Worster, *Dust Bowl*, p. 23.
47. Quoted in PBS Online, "Surviving the Dust Bowl."
48. Quoted in Watkins, *The Hungry Years*, pp. 429–30.
49. Quoted in Susan Chaffin, "Kansas in the Dust Bowl: 'We Aim to Stay,'" *Voices: The Kansas Collection Online Magazine*, Spring 1998. www.kancoll.org.

Chapter 3: In the Calm

50. Oral History Interviews.
51. Low, *Dust Bowl Diary*, p. 98.
52. Quoted in PBS Online, "Surviving the Dust Bowl."
53. Johnson, *Heaven's Tableland*, p. 177.
54. Low, *Dust Bowl Diary*, p. 49.
55. Oral History Interviews.
56. Oral History Interviews.
57. Oral History Interviews.
58. Oral History Interviews.
59. Oral History Interviews.
60. Oral History Interviews.
61. Low, *Dust Bowl Diary*, p. 37.
62. Low, *Dust Bowl Diary*, p. 156.
63. Oral History Interviews.
64. Oral History Interviews.
65. Oral History Interviews.
66. Oral History Interviews.
67. Oral History Interviews.
68. Oral History Interviews.
69. Herman Lawson, interview by author in Enumclaw, Washington, June 28, 2003.
70. Oral History Interviews.
71. Oral History Interviews.
72. Quoted in PBS Online, "Stories of Bob," *Frontline*, May 1, 1996. www.pbs.org.

Chapter 4: If It Rains

73. Quoted in PBS Online, "Surviving the Dust Bowl."
74. Glenn D. McMurry, "The Autobiography of an Unimportant Important Man," Resolution Productions, 1995. www.resolutionprod.com.
75. Low, *Dust Bowl Diary*, p. 127.
76. McMurry, "The Autobiography of an Unimportant Important Man."
77. Low, *Dust Bowl Diary*, p. 32.
78. Low, *Dust Bowl Diary*, p. 67.
79. Quoted in David Nichols, ed., *Ernie's America: The Best of Ernie Pyle's 1930s Travel Dispatches*. New York: Random House, 1989, p. 117.
80. Low, *Dust Bowl Diary*, p. 67.
81. Quoted in Bonnifield, *The Dust Bowl*, p. 194.
82. Quoted in PBS Online, "Surviving the Dust Bowl."
83. Oral History Interviews.
84. Quoted in PBS Online, "Surviving the Dust Bowl."
85. Oral History Interviews.
86. Oral History Interviews.
87. Quoted in *Countryside Magazine*, "Dusting Off Our Roots: The Dirty Thirties," March/April 2000. www.countrysidemag.com.
88. Quoted in Bonnifield, *The Dust Bowl*, pp. 72–73.
89. Quoted in PBS Online, "Surviving the Dust Bowl."
90. Quoted in PBS Online, "Surviving the Dust Bowl."

91. Quoted in Worster, *Dust Bowl*, p. 23.
92. Quoted in Watkins, *The Hungry Years*, p. 430.
93. Quoted in Hurt, *The Dust Bowl*, p. 58.
94. Woody Guthrie, "Dust Can't Kill Me," Ballads from Deep Gap, NC, and Okemah, OK; the Unofficial Doc and Merle Watson and Semi-Official Woody Guthrie and Almanac Singers Site, 2001. www.geocities.com.
95. Quoted in Linda Dzuris, "Using Folk Songs and Ballads in an Interdisciplinary Approach to American History," Society for History Education, May 2003. www.historycoop.org.
96. Oral History Interviews.

Chapter 5: Dusted Out

97. Quoted in PBS Online, "Surviving the Dust Bowl."
98. Quoted in PBS Online, "Surviving the Dust Bowl."
99. Oral History Interviews.
100. Quoted in PBS Online, "Stories of Bob."
101. Oral History Interviews.
102. Oral History Interviews.
103. Worster, *Dust Bowl*, p. 49.
104. Oral History Interviews.
105. Oral History Interviews.
106. Richard "Bud" Caudle, "The Great Depression: The Real Grapes of Wrath," RootsWeb.com, July 18, 2000. http://archiver.rootsweb.com.
107. Lawson interview, June 28, 2003.
108. Oral History Interviews.
109. Oral History Interviews.
110. Quoted in Watkins, *The Hungry Years*, p. 436.
111. Oral History Interviews.
112. Quoted in Watkins, *The Hungry Years*, p. 436.
113. Oral History Interviews.
114. Oral History Interviews.
115. Oral History Interviews.
116. Oral History Interviews.
117. Oral History Interviews.
118. Oral History Interviews.
119. Quoted in Watkins, *The Hungry Years*, p. 452.
120. Quoted in Watkins, *The Hungry Years*, p. 455.
121. Weedpatch Camp, "Personal Reminiscences of the Risner Family," n.d. www.weedpatchcamp.com.
122. Oral History Interviews.
123. Oral History Interviews.
124. New Deal Network, 2002, "On Drought Conditions." Roosevelt's Fireside Chats, September 6, 1936. www.newdeal.feri.org.

Chapter 6: To Help or Hinder

125. Worster, *Dust Bowl*, p. 35.
126. Quoted in Hurt, *The Dust Bowl*, p. 56.
127. Quoted in Hurt, *The Dust Bowl*, p. 56.
128. Quoted in Bonnifield, *The Dust Bowl*, p. 189.
129. New Deal Network, "On Drought Conditions."
130. *Worster, Dust Bowl*, pp. 128–29.
131. Oral History Interviews.
132. Low, *Dust Bowl Diary*, p. 109.
133. Low, *Dust Bowl Diary*, p. 117.
134. Quoted in Watkins, *The Hungry Years*, p. 351.
135. Quoted in Watkins, *The Hungry Years*, p. 433.
136. Oral History Interviews.
137. Quoted in Joseph Geringer, "Charles Arthur Floyd: The 'Pretty Boy' from Cookson Hills," Crime Library.com, 2003. www.crimelibrary.com.
138. Quoted in Geringer, "Charles Arthur Floyd: The 'Pretty Boy' from Cookson Hills."
139. Geringer, "Charles Arthur Floyd: The

'Pretty Boy' from Cookson Hills."

140. Quoted in Joseph Geringer, "Bonnie and Clyde: Romeo and Juliet in a Getaway Car," Crime Library.com, 2003. www.crimelibrary.com.

141. Quoted in PBS Online, "Surviving the Dust Bowl."

Chapter 7: The Dust Settles

142. Quoted in PBS Online, "Surviving the Dust Bowl."

143. Quoted in PBS Online, "Surviving the Dust Bowl."

144. Quoted in PBS Online, "Surviving the Dust Bowl."

145. Quoted in PBS Online, "Surviving the Dust Bowl."

146. Quoted in Worster, *Dust Bowl*, p. 214.

147. Quoted in Johnson, *Heaven's Tableland*, p. 246.

148. American Presidency Project, 2003, "Address at Ellwood Park, Amarillo, Texas," July 11, 1938. www.presidency.ucsb.edu.

149. Quoted in Bonnifield, *The Dust Bowl*, pp. 85–86.

150. Quoted in PBS Online, "Surviving the Dust Bowl."

151. Oral History Interviews.

152. Oral History Interviews.

153. Oral History Interviews.

154. Oral History Interviews.

155. Quoted in Worster, *Dust Bowl*, p. 162.

156. Quoted in Johnson, *Heaven's Tableland*, p. 241.

157. Johnson, *Heaven's Tableland*, pp. 264–65.

158. Lawson interview, June 28, 2003.

159. Quoted in Adams County Historical Society, "The Dust Bowl Years," 2002. www.rootsweb.com.

160. Oral History Interviews.

161. Oral History Interviews.

162. Oral History Interviews.

163. Quoted in Johnson, *Heaven's Tableland*, pp. 273–74.

Epilogue: Another Dust Bowl?

164. Quoted in Dennis T. Avery, "Another Dust Bowl . . . or Just Blowing Smoke?" Center for Global Food Issues, August 9, 2002. www.cgfi.com.

165. Quoted in Mary Jane Dunlap, "Dust Bowl Lessons: KU Historian Reviews What 'Dirty '30s' Taught Americans," University of Kansas, Office of University Relations, March 3, 2003. www.ur. ku.edu.

166. Quoted in Randy Francis, "The Texas Dust Bowl in Historical Perspective: What Happened and Could It Happen Again?" John Cletheroe's Personal Website, June 1998. http://freespace.virgin.net.

167. Quoted in PBS Online, "Surviving the Dust Bowl."

168. Farm Service Agency, U.S. Department of Agriculture, "Preparing for Drought in the 21st Century," *National Drought Policy Commission Report*, May 2000. www.fsa.usda.gov.

169. Hurt, *The Dust Bowl*, p. 159.

170. Quoted in Bonnifield, *The Dust Bowl*, p. 202.

For Further Reading

Books

Tricia Andryszewski, *The Dust Bowl: Disaster on the Plains*. Brookfield, CT: Millbrook Press, 1993. An overview of the dust bowl.

Jacqueline Farrell, *The Great Depression*. San Diego: Lucent Books, 1996. An account of the Great Depression that affected the United States in the 1930s.

Milton Meltzer, *Driven From the Land: The Story of the Dust Bowl*. Tarrytown, NY: Marshall Cavendish, 2000. The story of the dust bowl with an emphasis on those who migrated to California.

Petra Press, *The 1930s: A Cultural History of the United States Through the Decades*. San Diego: Lucent Books, 1999. A look at life in the United States in the 1930s.

Internet

Arvin Federal Government Camp, "The Weedpatch Camp," 2003. www.weedpatchcamp.com. Photos and information about one of the government camps set up for dust bowl migrants in California.

Oral History Interviews, Dust Bowl Migration Digital Archives, California State University Bakersfield Library, 2003. www.lib.csub.edu. The site includes numerous detailed interviews with dust bowl residents who migrated to California in the 1930s.

PBS Online, "Surviving the Dust Bowl," *The American Experience*, 1999. www.pbs.org. A great overview of the dust bowl. Includes interviews and period photos.

Works Consulted

Books

Paul Bonnifield, *The Dust Bowl: Men, Dirt, and Depression.* Albuquerque: University of New Mexico Press, 1979. An account of the dust bowl, based on personal interviews and local sources. Includes background chapters on the history of the plains.

Ezra Bowen, ed., *This Fabulous Century: 1920–1930.* New York: Time-Life Books, 1969. A superior overview of the 1920s, including dozens of period photos, advertising blurbs, tabloid articles, and other material.

R. Douglas Hurt, *The Dust Bowl: An Agricultural and Social History.* Chicago: Nelson-Hall, 1981. The book focuses on the causes of the dust bowl, the storms themselves, life in the dust bowl, agricultural problems, the Shelterbelt Project, and more. Includes period photos of the storms.

Peter Jennings and Todd Brewster, *The Century.* New York: Doubleday Dell, 1998. A chronicle of the twentieth century by a renowned broadcast journalist and a former editor of *Life* magazine.

Vance Johnson, *Heaven's Tableland: The Dust Bowl Story.* New York: Farrar, Straus, 1947. An early account of the dust bowl, concentrating on the farmers and the weather, which was the greatest controlling factor of their existence.

Ann Marie Low, *Dust Bowl Diary.* Lincoln: University of Nebraska Press, 1984. Reminiscences of a teen coming to maturity in southeastern North Dakota in the 1930s.

David Nichols, ed., *Ernie's America: The Best of Ernie Pyle's 1930s Travel Dispatches.* New York: Random House, 1989. A collection of newspaper columns written by famed journalist Ernie Pyle during the 1930s. Includes his observations on two trips through the dust bowl.

T.H. Watkins, *The Hungry Years: A Narrative History of the Great Depression in America.* New York: Henry Holt, 1999. A study of the Great Depression with sections on the dust bowl.

Donald Worster, *Dust Bowl: The Southern Plains in the 1930s.* Oxford: Oxford University Press, 1979. A factual account of the dust bowl by an author whose parents lived in the Great Plains during the 1930s.

Periodicals

Caroline A. Henderson, "Letters from the Dust Bowl," *Atlantic Monthly*, May 1936. Letters written from a farm woman in the dust bowl in 1935 to a friend in Maryland.

Michael Parfit, "The Dust Bowl," *Smithsonian*, June 1989. A well-written overview of the dust bowl. Asks the question, could the dust bowl happen all over again?

Interviews

Herman Lawson. Interviewed by author, Enumclaw, Washington, June 28, 2003. Lawson was nine years old when his family moved from Missouri to Bristow, Oklahoma, in 1934. He and his family migrated to Salem, Oregon, in 1938.

Internet Sources

Adams County Historical Society, "The Dust Bowl Years," 2002. www.rootsweb.com.

American Presidency Project, 2003, "Address at Ellwood Park, Amarillo, Texas," July 11, 1938. www.presidency.ucsb.edu.

H. Allen Anderson, "Ward A. Thornton," *The Handbook of Texas Online*, Texas State Historical Association, 2002. www.tsha. utexas.edu.

Dennis T. Avery, "Another Dust Bowl . . . or Just Blowing Smoke?" Center for Global Food Issues, August 9, 2002. www.cgfi. com.

Richard "Bud" Caudle, "The Great Depression: The Real Grapes of Wrath," RootsWeb.com, July 18, 2000. http:// archiver.rootsweb.com.

Susan Chaffin, "Kansas in the Dust Bowl: 'We Aim to Stay,'" *Voices: The Kansas Collection Online Magazine*, Spring 1998. www.kancoll.org.

Countryside Magazine, "Dusting Off Our Roots: The Dirty Thirties," March/April 2000. www.countrysidemag.com.

Mary Jane Dunlap, "Dust Bowl Lessons: KU Historian Reviews What 'Dirty '30s' Taught Americans," University of Kansas, Office of University Relations, March 3, 2003. www.ur.ku.edu.

Linda Dzuris, "Using Folk Songs and Ballads in an Interdisciplinary Approach to American History," Society for History Education, May 2003. www.historycoop.org.

Farm Service Agency, U.S. Department of Agriculture, "Preparing for Drought in the 21st Century," *National Drought Policy Commission Report*. May 2000. www. fsa.usda.gov.

Randy Francis, "The Texas Dust Bowl in Historical Perspective: What Happened and Could It Happen Again?" John Cletheroe's Personal Website, June 1998. http://free space.virgin.net.

Joseph Geringer, "Bonnie and Clyde: Romeo and Juliet in a Getaway Car," Crime Library.com, 2003. www.crimelibrary.com.

———, "Charles Arthur Floyd: The 'Pretty Boy' from Cookson Hills," Crime Library.com, 2003. www.crimelibrary. com.

Woody Guthrie, "Dust Can't Kill Me," Ballads from Deep Gap, NC, and Okemah, OK; the Unofficial Doc and Merle Watson and Semi-Official Woody Guthrie and Almanac Singers Site, 2001. www. geocities.com.

Glenn D. McMurry, "The Autobiography of an Unimportant Important Man," Resolution Productions, 1995. www.resolution prod.com.

Jan E. Morris, "Blasts from the Past: Bonnie and Clyde," Cinetropic, 2003. www.cine tropic.com.

Dave Mowitz, "History Warns of Another Dust Bowl," *Agriculture Online*, March 12, 1999. www.agriculture.com.

New Deal Network, 2002, "On Drought Conditions," Roosevelt's Fireside Chats, September 6, 1936. www.newdeal.feri.org.

PBS Online, "Stories of Bob," *Frontline*, May 1, 1996. www.pbs.org.

Lisa Levitt Ryckman, "Plains," *Denver Rocky Mountain News*, March 26, 1999. www. denver-rmn.com.

Weedpatch Camp, "Personal Reminiscences of the Risner Family," n.d. www.weed patchcamp.com.

Index

Picture Credits

Cover: © Hulton Archive by Getty Images
AP Wide World Photos, 11, 35, 37, 65, 86, 92
© Bettmann/CORBIS, 23, 26, 32, 39, 50, 54,
  57, 61, 74, 76, 77, 81, 83
© CORBIS, 36, 70
Corel Corporation, 20
© Hulton Archive by Getty Images, 28, 43,
  49, 58, 62

© Hulton-Deutsch Collection/CORBIS,
  18
Library of Congress, 16, 66, 85
Brandy Noon, 12
© Property of Blackbirch Press, 73
© Arthur Rothstein/CORBIS, 29
© A & J Verkaik/CORBIS, 46

About the Author

Diane Yancey is a freelance writer who has written more than twenty books for middle-grade and high school readers. Her works published by Lucent Books include *Life During the Roaring Twenties*, *Al Capone*, and *Al Capone's Chicago*.

Yancey and her husband live in the Pacific Northwest with their dog, Gelato. Yancey enjoys collecting old books, reading mysteries, and traveling.